# CRYPTO 101

## DEEP IN THE HEART OF TEXIT

**JAMES DUMAINE**

# ACKNOWLEDGMENTS

As this book comes to life, it would be incomplete without expressing deep gratitude to the individuals whose vision, courage, and faith laid the foundation for what Texit Coin has become.

**To Bobby Gray** — thank you for your unwavering integrity, your remarkable vision, and the bold leadership it took to create Texit Coin. Your work is a testament to what can be achieved when innovation meets courage, and your commitment continues to inspire a growing community.

**To Jeh Horton** — your passion as a leader and your ability to lead with both conviction and compassion has shaped the Texit Coin movement in profound ways. Thank you for setting a shining example of what it means to take intelligent risks in today's economic landscape. Your belief in people and possibilities is contagious.

**To Eddie Allan** — A sincere and personal thank you to **Eddie Allen** for being an unwavering resource during the onboarding journey of so many new miners. Your patience, clarity, and one-on-one support have helped bridge the gap for countless users who would have otherwise been left behind. You truly embody the spirit of community-driven innovation.

**To Mike Healy** — Equally heartfelt thanks to **Mike Healy** for his outstanding YouTube tutorials, which have made navigating the Texit Coin environment far more accessible. Your commitment to clear, helpful education has been a vital guidepost for countless users entering the ecosystem.

**To the support team** — every person who stepped forward to build the infrastructure, provide help, solve problems, and serve the Texit Coin mission behind the scenes: thank you. Your dedication, talent, and teamwork have transformed this project into an outstanding case study in decentralized collaboration.

**To the early miners** — your participation has shown the true essence of community: faith in a new idea, and kindness toward one another as you built together. You are pioneers in every sense, and your willingness to move forward in unity is the soul of this ecosystem.

To every coder, dreamer, miner, and teacher —This book is for you — and because of you.

# CONTENTS

# INTRODUCTION — MY STORY, YOUR START

Welcome. If you're reading this, you're already curious — and that's the best place to begin. My journey into cryptocurrency didn't start with charts, codes, or conferences. It started with a conversation.

I have met the **founder** of **Texit Coin (TXC)** and the **currency director** personally on several occasions. I got involved early, and I've watched from the inside as this incredible project took shape. What began as a small conversation among passionate Texans has now evolved into a real, functioning, utility-based cryptocurrency — with working hardware, coin value growth, and a big vision for the future.

You may feel overwhelmed. Maybe you've heard terms like *blockchain*, *mining*, *cold storage*, and *hash rate*, but they don't make sense yet. That's okay. This book is here to walk you through it all — in plain English, with real examples, and a focus on **Texit Coin**, our very own crypto project with big ambitions for the Lone Star State.

So buckle in. You've got your seat on the rocket ship. Let's explore this new frontier together.

But before we launch too far into the Texit Coin story, let's pause and ask a question that's on a lot of minds: *Is it a cryptocurrency world now?*

The short answer is — **not entirely, but we're headed that way.** Cryptocurrency may not have taken over every transaction yet, but it's becoming impossible to ignore. Here's why:

**Realities About the Cryptocurrency World**

1. **Over 400 million people worldwide own crypto** — and that number keeps growing.

2. **Major companies now accept cryptocurrency** for goods and services — from tech giants to fast food chains.

3. **Nations are exploring or launching digital currencies** — like China's digital yuan and discussions around a U.S. digital dollar.

4. **Blockchain technology is being adopted beyond money** — used in supply chains, healthcare, art, and even voting systems.

5. **Crypto is challenging traditional financial systems** — offering decentralized alternatives that don't rely on banks or governments.

6. **Volatility is real** — the crypto market can swing wildly, but so can its potential for returns.

7. **It's regulated differently everywhere** — from full bans to full adoption, depending on where you are.

8. **Education is still the biggest barrier** — most people still don't fully understand how crypto works or why it matters.

Now for the second question: *Is cryptocurrency important to banks?*

Absolutely — **and not just because it threatens their traditional role.**

Banks are watching the crypto space closely, and many are jumping in. Some are:

- **Building their own digital currencies (CBDCs)** to stay competitive.

- **Offering crypto investment options** to their clients.

- **Exploring blockchain** to improve how they clear payments or secure data.

- **Partnering with crypto companies** instead of competing with them outright.

In short: **crypto isn't just a fringe idea anymore.** It's reshaping money itself — how it moves, who controls it, and what it's worth. That's why this book matters, and that's why your curiosity is your most valuable asset right now.

# Why Multi-Level Marketing + Crowdfunding Is the Business Model of the 21st Century

In a world where trust in big institutions is crumbling and traditional job markets are unpredictable, people are looking for new ways to earn, build, and belong. That's where the hybrid model of **multi-level marketing (MLM)** combined with **crowdfunding dynamics** comes in — and why it's thriving in today's economy.

You might ask: *Why does this model work so well now?* Let's break it down.

### 1.   People Trust People, Not Corporations

In the age of social media and decentralized networks, word of mouth has replaced billboards. When a friend or family member introduces you to a project or product, it carries more weight than any ad campaign. MLM capitalizes on this — turning everyday people into ambassadors and stakeholders, not just customers.

### 2.   Everyone Wants Ownership and Access

Crowdfunding gave rise to a whole new generation of entrepreneurs and investors. People want **skin in the game** — not just to support something, but to be part of building it. This sense of coownership (financial or ideological) fuels loyalty, engagement, and viral growth.

### 3.   The Economy Is Gig-Driven

More people than ever are freelancing, side hustling, or trying to escape the 9-to-5 grind. This model meets them where they are. It offers **low-barrier entry**, **flexible participation**, and **potential income** for anyone who can build a community or share a compelling message.

### 4.   It's Built on Incentives, Not Just Hope

In MLM + crowdfunding hybrids, people are rewarded for more than just financial investment — they're rewarded for belief, action, and outreach. That changes the dynamic. The energy that used to go into advertising now goes into **rewarding community-building**, which feels more personal and ethical when done transparently.

### 5.  Technology Has Made It Seamless

Smart contracts, blockchain, peer-to-peer payments, referral tracking — the tools that make these models run used to be complicated or expensive. Now, they're built into platforms and wallets. That means it's **easier than ever to reward contributors, split revenue, and track impact transparently.**

### 6.  It Supports Underdogs and Niche Communities

This model allows passionate, underserved groups to rally around causes or innovations that traditional banks or VCs ignore. It decentralizes opportunity. Whether it's a local coin like Texit Coin or a new app for a small demographic, this model **gives power to the people** — quite literally.

In today's world, people don't just want to buy. They want to belong. They want to support things that reflect their values, grow their wealth, and connect them to others.

**That's why this model works.** It's not about selling — it's about sharing. It's not just about funding — it's about building movements. And in the economy we're living in now, **movements matter more than marketing.**

So as you read on, keep that in mind: the crypto revolution is not just technological — it's social. It's communal. And it's built on new models of trust, value, and participation that the old system just can't keep up with.

Let's explore how Texit Coin is tapping into all of that — and why it's not just a coin, but a cause.

## Why Traditional Retirement Plans Are Losing Their Power

First we need to understand, for decades, Americans were told the same story: work hard, pay your taxes, contribute to your 401(k), and when the time comes, you'll be able to retire comfortably. But that story is starting to fall apart — and people are waking up to a new reality.

## Social Security: A Cracking Foundation

Social Security was never meant to be a full retirement plan. It was designed as a safety net. But today, even that net is wearing thin.

Here's why Social Security is becoming unreliable:

- **Demographics are shifting.** Fewer workers are paying into the system while more retirees are drawing from it. That imbalance is unsustainable.

- **The trust fund is shrinking.** According to government reports, the Social Security trust fund could be depleted by the mid-2030s — after which only partial benefits may be paid unless Congress acts.

- **Inflation outpaces payments.** Even with cost-of-living adjustments, the monthly checks don't keep up with real-world price increases in healthcare, housing, and essentials.

- **You have no control.** It's a government-controlled system. You can't adjust it, improve it, or pull from it early. You're at the mercy of political decisions and economic forces.

## 401(k) Plans: Built on Shaky Ground

While 401(k)s offer tax advantages and employer matching, they're not the silver bullet they were once marketed to be.

Here's why 401(k) plans are less dependable today:

- **They're market-dependent.** Your future depends on how the stock market performs — and market volatility is more frequent and unpredictable than ever.

- **Fees eat into returns.** Many 401(k) plans come with hidden fees, management costs, and restrictions that reduce overall gains.

- **Withdrawals are inflexible.** Pulling money out early comes with penalties and taxes, and when you do retire, required withdrawals can affect your tax situation.

- **Not everyone gets employer matching.** Gig workers, freelancers, and many small business employees don't even have access to a solid 401(k) plan.

- **Inflation risk is real.** Even with investment growth, inflation can erode the actual purchasing power of your retirement savings.

**The truth?** The old systems were built for a different world — one where people stayed at one job for 30 years, bought a house in their 20s, and retired at 65 with a gold watch. That world doesn't exist anymore.

That's why people are looking for **new ways to build wealth, create passive income, and take ownership of their financial future.** This is where cryptocurrency — and especially community-based, utility-driven crypto like Texit Coin — becomes part of the modern solution.

Because in the new economy, *you can't afford to depend on the old playbook.*

# Retirement Isn't What It Used to Be — Because Most Can't Afford to Stop Working

Ok! One last thing before I get off my economic soapbox. We used to think of retirement as a time to relax — travel, spend time with grandkids, garden, maybe take up golf. But for millions of Americans, retirement looks very different now.

More and more people are finding that they simply can't afford to stop working. Not because they want to stay busy — but because **they need the income to survive.**

### The Hard Numbers

- As of recent studies, **over 40% of Americans aged 62 to 70 are still working** in some capacity.

- According to the U.S. Census Bureau, **nearly 1 in 5 Americans over age 65** is still working — the highest percentage in over 50 years.

- A survey by Transamerica found that **55% of retirees retire with debt**, and **only 27% believe they'll have enough to last through retirement.**

- The median retirement savings for those nearing retirement (ages 55–64) is just **$134,000**, which would generate less than **$500/month** in income for most — not nearly enough to cover rent, food, and healthcare.

## Real People, Real Struggles

**Sandra**, a 68-year-old grandmother in Arizona, retired from her job as a school secretary thinking her Social Security and modest 401(k) would be enough. Within two years, rising rent and medical bills forced her back into part-time work as a cashier — just to stay afloat.

**James**, a former factory worker in Ohio, retired at 62 after decades of manual labor. But with only Social Security and a small pension, he now drives for a ride-share company during the day and delivers food at night.

**Maria and David**, a retired couple in Florida, sold their home to downsize, thinking they could live on their savings. But inflation and medical expenses ate into their budget so fast, they now run a small Etsy business just to supplement their income.

These are not exceptions — they're the new normal.

## The System Isn't Built to Carry You Anymore

- Pensions are rare.

- Costs are up.

- Lifespans are longer.

- Health issues are common.

- And most retirement plans were built on the assumption that you wouldn't need income for more than 10–15 years after retiring. That's outdated thinking.

In other words: **retirement has become a second career for many people — and not by choice.**

That's why people are turning to **alternative income strategies** like cryptocurrency, referral programs, digital investing, and community-led wealth building. They're realizing that if the system won't take care of them, **they have to build a new one themselves.**

And that's what this book — and Texit Coin — is really about: creating something sustainable, accessible, and community-driven for those who refuse to retire into poverty.

Because hope is not a strategy. But **action is.**

Let's keep going — because once you understand where cryptocurrency is headed, you'll see exactly why Texit Coin is more than just another digital currency. It's a movement, and you're now part of it.

# CHAPTER 1 – UNDERSTANDING CRYPTOCURRENCY

## What is Cryptocurrency?

Cryptocurrency is a **digital or virtual form of money** that uses cryptography for security. Unlike traditional currencies issued by governments (like the U.S. Dollar or Euro), cryptocurrencies operate on decentralized networks based on **blockchain technology**.

A **blockchain** is a distributed ledger that records all transactions across a network of computers. Each block in the chain contains a list of transactions, and once a block is full, it is added to the chain, making it immutable and secure.

Some popular examples of cryptocurrency include:

- **Bitcoin (BTC)**

- **Ethereum (ETH)**

- **Litecoin (LTC)**

- **Texit Coin (TXC)**

TXC is the cryptocurrency that we'll be focusing on throughout this course, and it's unique because it is designed for **real-world use** — specifically, to be used in local Texas economies as a utility coin.

## How Does Cryptocurrency Work?

Cryptocurrency operates through a system known as **mining**. Mining is the process by which new coins are created and transactions are added to the blockchain.

There are two key parts to mining:

1.  **Transaction Verification**: Each time someone sends or receives cryptocurrency, the transaction is verified by the network. Miners validate these transactions by solving complex mathematical puzzles, which requires significant computational power.

2.  **Block Creation**: When a miner successfully solves a puzzle, they get to add a new block to the blockchain. In return, they are rewarded with a certain amount of cryptocurrency (like **Bitcoin**, **Ethereum**, or **TXC**).

## What is a Hash Rate?

Now, let's dive into a critical term in mining: **hash rate**.

A **hash rate** is the measure of a miner's **computational power**. It refers to how many **hashes** (mathematical calculations) a miner's computer can perform per second while attempting to solve the puzzle that will add a block to the blockchain.

Here's a more technical explanation:

*   A **hash** is a cryptographic output, generated by a hashing algorithm. It is a fixed-length string of numbers and letters. In the case of **Bitcoin**, the algorithm is **SHA-256**, while **Ethereum** uses **Ethash**.

*   The **hash rate** is the number of times per second a miner can compute these hashes.

The higher the **hash rate**, the more calculations the mining machine can process in a given period. This leads to **faster block creation** and increases the likelihood of earning cryptocurrency rewards.

For example:

*   A **10 TH/s** hash rate means the miner can perform **10 trillion hashes per second**.

*   A **1 MH/s** hash rate means the miner can perform **1 million hashes per second**.

## Why Does Hash Rate Matter?

The **hash rate** is crucial because it directly impacts the **mining speed** and **security** of the network:

1. **Mining Speed**: The more powerful the miner's hardware (higher hash rate), the faster they can solve blocks and earn rewards.

2. **Network Security**: A high combined hash rate across the entire network ensures that it's **difficult** for malicious actors to manipulate the blockchain, making it more secure.

When it comes to **Texit Coin (TXC)**, the goal is to have a strong, **consistent hash rate** to keep the mining operation secure and to generate a significant number of coins over time. This is why TXC mining operations rely on powerful mining machines (ASICs) and crowd-funded shares, so that the total hash rate can be maximized to produce a steady coin output.

## Mining vs. Buying Cryptocurrency

Now that we understand the concept of mining and hash rate, let's compare **mining** to **buying** cryptocurrency:

- **Mining** involves using computational power to solve problems and validate transactions on the blockchain, thus earning newly created coins. As a miner, you invest in **mining equipment** (like ASICs or GPUs) and **electricity**, and your earnings depend on factors like **hash rate** and the current mining difficulty.

- **Buying** cryptocurrency, on the other hand, means purchasing coins directly from an exchange using traditional currency or another crypto. You don't need to own mining equipment, and you're essentially buying the asset at market price.

With **Texit Coin**, both options are available:

- You can **mine TXC** through the shared mining system. Essentially it is set up as a crowdfund structure.

- You can also **buy TXC** through exchanges like **BitMart**, **DexTrade**, and **MEXC**.

## The Role of TXC

**Texit Coin (TXC)** is designed to be more than just a speculative investment. It is **a utility coin**, with the goal of becoming widely used in local Texas economies for everyday transactions. By combining cryptocurrency with real-world applications, TXC aims to become **the official coin of Texas**.

The future of TXC is deeply connected to the **mining process**. As more people mine, the **hash rate** increases, helping to secure the network and ensure the **coin's stability and value**.

### Recap

- **Cryptocurrency** is digital money powered by blockchain.

- **Mining** is the process of earning coins through transaction verification and puzzlesolving.

- **Hash rate** measures the computational power used in mining.

- **Texit Coin (TXC)** is a **utility coin** aimed at transforming local economies in Texas.

## Crowdfunding and Texit Coin's Shared Mining Model

**Crowdfunding** is a method of raising capital through the collective effort of a large number of individuals, typically via the internet. It leverages the broad reach of social media and online platforms to pool small investments or contributions from a large group of people, bypassing traditional financial intermediaries. In the context of cryptocurrency, crowdfunding can serve as a powerful vehicle to launch projects, fund development, or decentralize ownership from the outset. It also fosters community involvement and early adoption, aligning supporters' financial interests with the success of the project.

**Texit Coin** adopts a unique form of crowdfunding through its **shared mining model**—a decentralized fundraising structure designed to distribute ownership and rewards across a broad base of participants. Instead of relying solely on venture capital or private investment, Texit Coin invites contributors to take part in mining operations from the very beginning. Through this model, supporters contribute computing power or financial resources toward a shared mining pool. In return, they receive proportional allocations of the mined Texit Coins based on their level of participation or investment.

This shared mining approach democratizes access to the coin generation process, turning early supporters into stakeholders and network participants. It also helps secure the blockchain by encouraging broad participation in the network's maintenance and validation processes. Unlike traditional ICOs (Initial Coin Offerings), which often concentrate tokens in the hands of a few investors, Texit Coin's crowdfunding model promotes decentralization, community ownership, and long-term engagement.

Ultimately, the Texit Coin shared mining structure is not just a funding mechanism—it is a foundational pillar of its community-centric ethos. It aligns economic incentives with the project's mission, enabling supporters to help build and benefit from a decentralized financial future, all while supporting the broader movement for economic independence symbolized by the Texit initiative.

## The War Between Plastic and Crypto

Credit card companies tend to view cryptocurrency transactions, like those involving Texit Coin, with caution and sometimes outright fear because they disrupt the traditional financial infrastructure these companies rely on. Texit Coin operates on a decentralized blockchain, which means transactions are peer-to-peer and recorded on an immutable ledger. Unlike credit card payments, which can be reversed in cases of fraud or disputes through chargebacks, Texit Coin transactions are final and irreversible. This lack of a safety net increases the financial risk for credit card companies, who are accustomed to protecting both themselves and consumers from fraudulent charges.

Moreover, Texit Coin's blockchain technology introduces a transparency paradox. While transactions are publicly recorded on the blockchain, the identities behind wallet addresses remain pseudonymous, making it difficult for credit card companies to perform the usual Know Your Customer (KYC) and Anti-Money

Laundering (AML) checks they rely on. This creates regulatory uncertainty, as credit card companies face potential liabilities if their platforms inadvertently facilitate illegal activities via cryptocurrencies like Texit Coin. Without the ability to fully monitor or control transactions, credit card companies feel exposed to reputational and legal risks.

Lastly, the highly volatile nature of cryptocurrencies such as Texit Coin further complicates matters. Price fluctuations can occur rapidly, meaning the value of a transaction can change drastically between the time a payment is initiated and settled. This instability makes it harder for credit card companies to manage their financial risk and reconcile transactions efficiently. Coupled with the ongoing evolution of government regulations around cryptocurrencies, credit card companies see transactions involving Texit Coin as a disruptive threat to their established business models, prompting them to proceed cautiously or restrict such payments altogether.

## Real-World Responses to Crypto — and Texit Coin's Implications

Credit card giants like **Visa**, **Mastercard**, and **American Express** have had a mixed relationship with cryptocurrency. While they've explored blockchain technologies and even partnered with crypto firms, they've also placed **strict limits or outright bans** on direct crypto purchases, especially through certain exchanges or wallets. For example, Mastercard temporarily blocked crypto transactions in several regions due to **fraud concerns and regulatory uncertainty**. These moves weren't just technical policy shifts — they reflected deep institutional anxiety over ceding control to decentralized systems.

Texit Coin, as a new entrant with a mission focused on **decentralization and financial sovereignty**, magnifies these concerns. So is Texit Coin safe? It goes without saying that in any investment opportunity there are risks. However, Texit Coin's DNA is based on the commitment to honest money using a currency designed to level the playing field for the purpose of fair value exchange according to the founders. If Texit Coin were to grow in popularity and start being used for everyday purchases — bypassing traditional banking rails — credit card networks would face a **loss of transaction volume**, fee revenue, and visibility into spending behavior. Since blockchain-based transactions can skip intermediary financial institutions altogether, every Texit Coin transaction is one that doesn't pass through the tollbooth of Visa or Mastercard's network.

In a hypothetical scenario, suppose a major e-commerce platform begins accepting Texit Coin directly through wallet integrations. Shoppers could then bypass credit cards entirely. Now, the platform avoids credit card processing fees, merchants get quicker settlements, and users maintain privacy. But for credit card companies, this is an existential threat — it erodes their relevance and undermines the infrastructure they've spent decades building.

The real kicker is compliance. If a user buys Texit Coin on a regulated exchange, then uses it to purchase digital goods — and those goods are later tied to illicit activity — who's liable? In traditional card networks, fraud and chargeback systems create a buffer. In Texit Coin's world, liability is murkier. Credit card companies fear being pulled into **regulatory crossfire**, especially in regions with strict anti-money-laundering mandates. This fear has led to **proactive blacklisting** of crypto merchants or wallet services — not necessarily because of wrongdoing, but due to perceived risk.

# CHAPTER 2 — MINING VS BUYING: TWO PATHS TO CRYPTO

MINING VS BUYING:
TWO PATHS TO CRYPTO

### 1. Buying Crypto
- Quick and easy
- No technical setup needed

**Pros:**
- Quick and easy
- No technical setup needed

**Cons:**
- You pay market prices
- You're relying on external platforms

### 2. Mining Crypto
Earning conns conduet computing power to the blockchain netwerk — a digital miner tat solves compex math proments

**Proof of Work**
You're ralying on

### My Setup (A Real-World Example)
Mining → Tether Wallet → Coinbase → Cold Storage Coin

### Buying vs Mining: Which is Right for You

| Feature | BUYING | MINING | MINING |
|---|---|---|---|
| Technical Skill Needed | Low (flexible (at $10) | Flexible (hardware) | Higher (mnitial (harbare/share costs) |
| Risk Level | Medium (fluctuations) | Medium–High (hardwars, electricity) | Steady passive accumulation |

When entering the world of cryptocurrency, two primary roads lie ahead: **buying** or **mining**. Each has its own tools, risks, and rewards. Understanding both is essential to knowing where you fit in the blockchain ecosystem.

## 1. Buying Crypto

Buying is the easiest and fastest way to get crypto. You exchange fiat currency (USD, EUR, etc.) for tokens like **BTC, ETH, USDT**, or **Texit Coin (TXC)** via centralized or decentralized exchanges.

### ◆ How it Works:

- Create an account on a crypto exchange (e.g., **Coinbase**, **Dex-Trade**, **Binance**)

- Link your bank account or credit card

- Purchase cryptocurrency directly

### ✅ Pros:

- Quick access to crypto

- No technical expertise required

- Ideal for first-time users or investors

## ✖ Cons:

- Subject to exchange fees and market volatility

- No control over platform downtime or withdrawal restrictions

- You don't *earn* the crypto — you're buying it at someone else's price

# ⛏ 2. Mining Crypto

Mining means **earning crypto** through computational effort. It's not just about buying coins, it's about **generating value** for the blockchain and being rewarded for it.

## ◆ What Is Mining?

In Proof of Work (PoW) systems like Bitcoin, miners solve complex math problems to verify blockchain transactions. In return, they're rewarded with newly minted coins.

## 🖥 Types of Mining Equipment:

- **ASICs** – Custom machines for mining one type of coin efficiently

- **GPUs** – Graphics cards often used to mine Ethereum and other altcoins

- **Cloud Mining** – Renting mining power from a provider instead of owning hardware

## 🤝 My Setup (A Real-World Example)

When I joined the Texit Coin ecosystem, I didn't just buy TXC. I bought a **mining share** — a virtual stake in a real machine housed in a secured facility. Here's what came with it:

- A **Tether (USDT) wallet** to collect rewards

- A linked **Coinbase account** to manage cash conversions

- A **cold storage TXC coin** to hold mined Texit Coin securely

Every day, the mining share generated TXC, which was sent directly to my wallet — **automatically, with no interaction needed**.

## 🔀 Buying vs Mining: Which is Right for You?

| Feature | Buying | Mining |
|---|---|---|
| Technical Skill Needed | Low | Medium to High |
| Initial Cost | Flexible (as low as $10) | Higher (hardware or share costs) |
| Risk Level | Medium (market fluctuations) | Medium-High (hardware, electricity, coin value) |
| Profit Source | Market price increase | Steady passive accumulation |
| Control | Rely on 3rd-party exchange | Direct interaction with blockchain |

## 💡 Consider This

Mining is often more profitable long-term for believers in the coin, especially with **TXC's earlystage mining incentives** and **cold wallet security**.

Buying is better if you want **liquidity**, **speed**, and **simplicity**.

You can also **combine both strategies**:

- Buy TXC now while prices are early-stage

- Invest in mining shares to grow your holdings passively

### 🧠 Bonus Insight: What Is "Proof of Work"?

Proof of Work (PoW) is the original consensus model used by Bitcoin. It ensures fairness, security, and decentralization by requiring computational effort to validate transactions. While energy-intensive, it's extremely secure — and it powers how you earn TXC through mining.

# CHAPTER 3 — THE POWER OF THE BLOCKCHAIN

## THE POWER OF THE BLOCKCHAIN

**Blockchain** is at the heart of everything crytso'3 revutionary way to store. verify, and encure information over a decentralized network.

### WHAT IS A BLOKCHAIN?

No one can alter recrooirs without altering every copy worldwide. E-ch entry αs"c o or a blocks. one yeamanontly linked to the one belfore it. This creates an luncangeisle history, known as the biockchain.

### HOW A BLOCK FORMED

| | |
|---|---|
| Transaction proposed | Measures miner or network power. |
| Transparent | Miners, combining. partners. share rewards |
| Proof of Work | Proof of Work (PoW) Rearitizes com— |
| Node | Computer on the blockchain, stores cks. |
| Gas Fees | Small payments to miners for processing transactions |

### DID YOU KNOW?

- In 2008, the psuedonymouSatoshi Nakamoto introduced Bircein and the blockchain concept
- In 2015, Ethercum αvgrade to Ethercum enabled complex applications through smart contracts

**SMART CONTRACT**

**Hash iate** – Measures miner or network forvources. Mning "

**Proof of Work** (PoW)/ Pow): Requiretes computatlonal effort for transactions and network

**Node** – A computer on the blockchain stores and verines blocks

**Gas Fees** – Smart payments to miners for processing

---

Blockchain is the invisible engine driving the entire world of cryptocurrency. It's not just a buzzword — it's a revolutionary way to store, verify, and secure information across a decentralized network.

## What Is a Blockchain?

Imagine a giant notebook, copied thousands of times and distributed across a global network of computers. Every time a transaction occurs, a new "entry" is added — and **everyone updates their copy**.

Each entry is called a **block**, and each block is permanently linked to the one before it. This creates an **unchangeable history**, known as the **blockchain**.

## Why It Matters

| Feature | What It Means |
|---|---|
| **Immutable** | No one can alter previous records without altering every copy worldwide. |
| **Transparent** | Anyone can see the transaction history. No hidden databases. |
| **Decentralized** | No central authority owns it — it runs on thousands of nodes globally. |
| **Secure** | Encrypted, verified, and virtually unhackable thanks to cryptographic hashes. |

## Real-World Example: The Blockchain in Action

Let's say you send 100 TXC to a friend. Here's what happens:

1. You sign the transaction with your private key.

2. The transaction is broadcast to the network.

3. Computers (miners) verify it using mathematical puzzles.

4. Once verified, it's added to the next block.

5. That block is linked to the previous one — forever.

You don't need to trust a middleman. The system itself proves the transaction.

# Terms to Know (Expanded)

- **Hash Rate** – Measures the power of a miner or network. Higher hash rates = faster problem-solving.

- **Mining Pool** – Miners combine resources to improve success rates and share rewards.

- **Proof of Work (PoW)** – Requires computational effort to validate transactions and secure the network.

- **Node** – A computer on the blockchain network that stores and helps verify blocks.

- **Gas Fees** – Small payments made to miners for processing transactions (common in Ethereum).

## Did You Know?

- The **Bitcoin blockchain** adds a block every ~10 minutes.

- The **Ethereum blockchain** does it every 12–15 seconds.

- **Over 450 million transactions** have been recorded on Ethereum since launch.

## Bonus Concept: Smart Contracts

Smart contracts are **self-executing agreements** written into code and stored on the blockchain. When conditions are met, the contract executes automatically — no lawyer, no banker.

Example:

"If James sends 100 TXC to the contract, then Rebecca receives it in her wallet — instantly."

### 🔒 Blockchain Isn't Just About Money

It's being used for:

- **Healthcare** (secure medical records)

- **Supply chains** (track goods from farm to store)

- **Voting** (tamper-proof digital ballots)

- **Digital identity** (verifying credentials)

### 📈 How a Block Is Formed

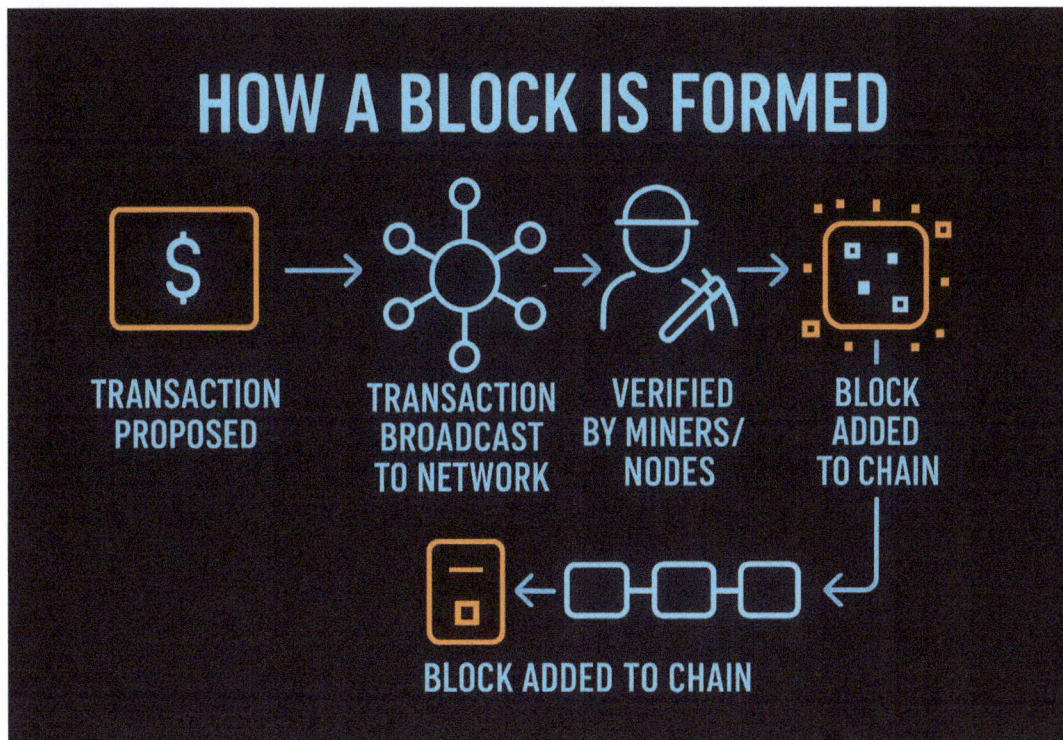

HOW A BLOCK IS FORMED

TRANSACTION PROPOSED → TRANSACTION BROADCAST TO NETWORK → VERIFIED BY MINERS/NODES → BLOCK ADDED TO CHAIN

BLOCK ADDED TO CHAIN

**How a Block Is Formed: Step-by-Step Explanation**

The formation of a block on the blockchain follows a secure and highly structured process. It begins when a **transaction is proposed**—for example, someone sends a cryptocurrency like TXC to another user. This transaction includes important details such as the sender's and receiver's wallet addresses, the amount being sent, and a timestamp. Once submitted, the **transaction is broadcast to the entire blockchain network**, where it is visible to thousands of decentralized computers, also known as nodes.

Next, the transaction enters the **verification phase**. Specialized participants called miners (in Proof of Work systems) or validators (in Proof of Stake systems) check the transaction for accuracy. They ensure that the sender has enough funds and that the transaction meets network rules. In the case of Proof of Work, this verification involves solving a complex mathematical puzzle. Once verified, the transaction is **added to a block** alongside other validated transactions.

This block is then assigned a unique digital fingerprint called a **cryptographic hash**, which ties it to the previous block in the chain. Once the block is complete and validated by consensus across the network, it is **added to the blockchain**—a permanent, immutable record that is distributed across all participating nodes. This system ensures trust, transparency, and security without requiring a central authority. Each new block strengthens the chain and preserves the integrity of every transaction that came before it.

# CHAPTER 4 — WHAT IS TEXIT COIN?

## A Homegrown Coin With a Bold Mission

**Texit Coin (TXC)** isn't just another cryptocurrency — it's a movement with a mission. Born in Texas, built by Texans, and designed to serve Texas and beyond, TXC is a **Layer 1** cryptocurrency that's being developed to function as **real, usable money**.

In fact, it already has its first real-world use case: **The City of Gonzales, Texas**, has signed on to participate in the rollout of TXC as a **utility coin** — a form of cryptocurrency designed for **actual spending** in local economies, not just investing or speculation.

**"We call it a utility coin because the end goal is to actually use it like cash — for gas, groceries, and government services."**

## What Makes TXC Different?

While thousands of cryptocurrencies exist, very few are designed with **practical, everyday utility** in mind. Texit Coin stands out in several key ways:

- ✅ **Utility-Driven**: The goal is for TXC to be used for real transactions — buying, selling, paying.

- ✅ **Layer 1 Blockchain**: This means it's built from the ground up on its own independent blockchain (not riding on another coin's system).

- ✅ **Mined, Not Minted**: TXC is mined like Bitcoin — using real hardware and energy — which gives it intrinsic production value.

- ✅ **Local-First Approach**: Starting in Gonzales, TX, with plans to expand across the state.

## The Vision for TXC

The long-term vision is to make **Texit Coin** a key player in local commerce, providing an **alternative financial system** for communities that want to reduce reliance on traditional banks and fiat currency.

Imagine walking into a store in Austin or Lubbock and paying with TXC. That's the goal.

## How TXC Works

### Mined Coin

- You can own mining shares.

- Each share gives you a daily portion of the TXC produced by the mine.

- The mine is planned to produce for **135 years** — that's long-term.

### Market Coin

- TXC is **currently trading** on:

  - DexTrade

  - MEXC

  - BitMart

- It launched at just **2.8¢** in **May 2025** and now trades around **$1.00 per coin** (as of late 2025).

**Community Coin**

- Referrals earn bonuses in mining power and even cash.

- The project is crowd-funded — everyone can own a piece of the mine and be part of the build.

## Transparency & Trust

Let's be real: there are a lot of scammy projects in crypto. The Texit Coin team knows this and has **gone out of its way to be transparent**.

- All mining results and metrics are published online.

- Every wallet, payment, and update is trackable.

- If you have questions, there's a **full support system** ready to help. help.mineTXC.com is your go-to resource.

## Quick Recap: Why TXC?

| Feature | TXC Strength |
|---|---|
| Layer 1 Blockchain | ✅ Yes |
| Utility Use Case | ✅ In Gonzales, TX and growing |
| Real Mining | ✅ Yes – not just tokens |
| Transparent Model | ✅ All data available |

| | | |
|---|---|---|
| ROI Since August | ✅ | ~500% growth |
| Crowd-Owned Mine | ✅ | You can join in |
| Trading Platforms | ✅ | DexTrade, MEXC, BitMart |

## The Adventure Awaits

If you're reading this, you're not just watching from the sidelines — you're in the early stages of a real financial evolution. TXC isn't just about making money; it's about building **something that lasts** — a **Texas-born financial alternative** backed by blockchain technology.

Coming up next: we'll dive into **how to mine TXC**, how you can earn it daily, and what it means to own a piece of the digital frontier.

**Let's continue now with Chapter 5: Mining Texit Coin – Your Digital Gold Mine. This is where we dig into how Texit Coin is mined, how you earn from it, and what it means to own a share in this groundbreaking digital operation.**

*NOTE: As we continue with this course, we'll explore how you can mine TXC, store it safely, and even use it in real-world scenarios. For now, keep in mind that understanding hash rate and how mining works gives you the foundation for deeper engagement with the Texit Coin ecosystem.*

# CHAPTER 5 — MINING TEXIT COIN: YOUR DIGITAL GOLD MINE

## What Is Crypto Mining?

Crypto mining is the process of using computer power to solve complex mathematical problems that validate and record transactions on a blockchain. As a reward for doing this work, miners are paid in cryptocurrency.

Think of mining as the **engine** that keeps the blockchain running — and the miners as the mechanics who keep the engine in top shape. Without miners, the blockchain would stop processing transactions.

### ASIC: The Modern Pickaxe

In the early days of crypto, you could mine Bitcoin using a regular laptop. Not anymore.

Now, we use a device called an **ASIC** — short for **Application-Specific Integrated Circuit**. It's a powerful computer built for one job: mining cryptocurrency. Unlike your laptop, which can run email, music, and games, an ASIC is laser-focused on solving blockchain problems quickly and efficiently.

**The faster your ASIC, the more crypto you mine.**

## How Does TXC Mining Work?

Texit Coin is a **Proof-of-Work** cryptocurrency — like Bitcoin. This means it relies on computational work (done by your miner) to secure the network and release new TXC coins.

Here's what that looks like in action:

1. You buy a **share** in the TXC mine.

2. That share gives you a **portion of the daily TXC production**.

3. Your coins are deposited into your **cold storage wallet** or **Tether account**, depending on your setup.

4. The mine continues to run, earning you TXC every single day.

**How Long Will It Mine?**

The mine is built to operate for a whopping **135 years**. That's not a typo. The mine is structured with long-term sustainability in mind — and the software automatically adjusts mining difficulty and rewards over time.

It's like owning a digital oil well — but instead of barrels of oil, you're collecting digital currency every day.

## Mining Performance and ROI

Let's talk results.

Since launching in **March 2025**, and with public mining beginning around **May**, the coin rose from **$0.028** to **$1.00** — that's a **3,471% price increase**. But it doesn't stop there.

Because you're not just holding a coin — you're earning **more coins every day** through mining.

That's why early adopters are already seeing **~500% returns on their initial mining share investment**, as of late 2025.

# Why Mining Over Buying?

You might ask: why not just buy TXC on an exchange and skip the mining part?

Fair question — and the answer depends on your goals.

| Method | Pros | Cons |
| --- | --- | --- |
| **Buying** | Simple, fast, good for short-term trading | You pay market price; no passive income |
| **Mining** | Earn daily coin, long-term passive returns, early access to lower costs | Requires upfront investment and setup time |

With mining, you **own part of the system** — and that can pay off in big ways over time.

# Cold Storage and Secure Coin Delivery

When you buy a mining share, your coins are delivered to you using a physical device: a **cold storage coin**. This is a secure, offline wallet that holds your TXC in a completely hack-proof form.

Here's how it works:

- The coin comes with a **QR code** on the back.

- Scan it using the **Blockchain Mint App** to see your TXC balance in real time.

- **IMPORTANT:** Once the cold wallet is opened, it is no longer considered secure. Always plan to transfer your funds and order a new cold wallet after use.

**Tip from Experience:** I'm currently waiting on a new cold wallet. Once it arrives, I'll transfer some of my TXC to **Tether** (a stablecoin), then move the rest back into the new cold wallet for long-term safety — and cash out the remaining balance. It's fast, simple, and secure.

## Referral Bonuses and Power-Ups

The mine also offers **referral rewards**. If you bring in new participants:

- You earn **extra mine power** (meaning more TXC daily)

- You may qualify for **cash bonuses** as well

This turns your mining share into a mini-business if you want it to — though this part is optional.

**Your Digital Mining Share: A Quick Recap**

- ✅ One-time purchase of a **mining share**

- ✅ Earn **daily TXC payouts**

- ✅ Real hardware, real coins

- ✅ Long-term operation: **135 years**

- ✅ Coins go straight to your **secure cold wallet**

- ✅ Referral bonuses available

## Mining Infrastructure and Technical Operations of Texit Coin

The mining backbone of **Texit Coin** is built on a sophisticated and energy-efficient computational infrastructure, currently housed in **McKinney, Texas**, with planned expansions into other areas of the **DFW metroplex** and across the state. Unlike many traditional mining operations that rely on outdated and power-hungry systems, Texit Coin employs **specialized mining rigs**—primarily **Application-Specific Integrated Circuits (ASICs)**—that are optimized specifically for the cryptographic hash functions used in blockchain mining.

These ASIC machines are capable of performing **trillions of cryptographic calculations per second (tera-hashes per second, or TH/s)**, providing the necessary computational strength to maintain the security and integrity of the Texit Coin blockchain. By distributing mining workloads across multiple high-performance units, the system achieves both **processing redundancy** and **network stability**, ensuring consistent block validation and resistance to central points of failure.

One of the standout technical innovations in Texit Coin's mining operation is its **immersive cooling system**. To address the significant heat generated by high-performance mining hardware, the rigs are **fully submerged in non-conductive dielectric oil**. This oil not only absorbs heat efficiently but also eliminates the need for traditional air-based cooling systems that involve loud fans or compressor-driven HVAC units.

The heat-laden oil is circulated through a **closed-loop cooling cycle**, where it is passively cooled by **quiet, low-energy fans** that dissipate heat through radiators or heat exchangers. This approach results in several benefits:

- **Minimal electricity usage** compared to air-cooled or compressor-based systems,

- **Virtually silent operation**, preventing noise pollution in residential or urban areas,

- **Extended hardware lifespan** due to reduced thermal stress.

By keeping the operational footprint discreet and environmentally conscious, Texit Coin mining facilities can be integrated into more diverse community settings without causing disruption—a strategic advantage as the network scales.

As the number of mining units grows and more locations come online, the **aggregate hash rate** will increase, enhancing the overall **network security** and **transaction processing capacity**. A geographically distributed and computationally diverse mining network also reduces the risk of downtime or regional power interruptions affecting operations. This layered expansion strategy supports both **technical resilience** and **decentralization**, aligning with the core principles of Texit Coin's mission.

## 🔐 1. Validate Transactions (Consensus Mechanism)

**Purpose:**

To confirm that a transaction on the blockchain is **legitimate** and hasn't been tampered with or double-spent.

**What's Calculated:**

- **Transaction verification**: Miners check digital signatures and balances.
- **Block creation**: Verified transactions are grouped into a new block.

## 🧮 2. Solve Cryptographic Hash Puzzles (Proof of Work)

**Purpose:**

To secure the blockchain by making it computationally expensive to add new blocks, thereby preventing fraud or manipulation.

**What's Calculated:**

- Miners repeatedly run the **SHA-256 hashing algorithm** (or other algorithms, depending on the blockchain) on a block's header.
- They aim to find a **hash output** (a string of numbers and letters) that meets strict criteria —typically, it must start with a certain number of **leading zeros**.

🔄 This process involves **trillions of guesses per second**, as miners change a variable called the **nonce** and hash again and again until they find a valid result.

## 3. Maintain Consensus and Blockchain Integrity

**Purpose:**

To ensure all participants agree on the current state of the blockchain (called **consensus**), without needing a central authority.

**What's Calculated:**

- **Longest valid chain** detection: Miners and nodes calculate which chain of blocks is the longest and has the most Proof of Work.

- **Fork resolution**: In case of chain splits, miners compute which version of the chain to continue working on.

## 4. Generate New Coins (Block Rewards)

**Purpose:**

To introduce new cryptocurrency into circulation and reward miners for their efforts.

**What's Calculated:**

- Once a miner finds a valid hash, they add the new block to the blockchain and receive a **block reward**—a fixed number of new coins (e.g., Texit Coin).

- They also collect **transaction fees** from the transactions included in that block.

## 🔧 Example of a Hash Calculation (Simplified):

A miner might hash this block header data:

```yaml
CopyEdit
Previous block hash: 000000...
Transactions: [Tx1, Tx2, Tx3...]
Timestamp: 2025-05-29
Nonce: 10432948 Until it
finds a SHA-256 hash like:
```

```scss
CopyEdit
000000abcd4358c394... (meets difficulty target)
```

## 📊 Summary of Mining Calculations

| Function | Algorithm Used | Purpose |
| --- | --- | --- |
| Hash Puzzle Solving | SHA-256 (or others) | Secures network (Proof of Work) |
| Transaction Validation | Digital signatures | Ensures correctness and prevents fraud |
| Chain Consensus | Cumulative work check | Maintains a single trusted ledger |
| Reward Calculation | Blockchain logic | Distributes coins and fees |

**Next Chapter: Managing Your Crypto – Wallets, Tether, and Staying Safe**

Now that you know how the mining works and coins are earned, it's time to learn **how to manage, protect, and transfer** your TXC like a pro.

We'll cover **hot vs cold wallets**, **stablecoins**, and the **best practices for keeping your crypto safe** — especially if you plan to cash out or reinvest.

Ready for **Chapter 6: Wallets – Hot, Cold, and Secure**?

Let's move into **Chapter 6**, where we break down wallets, safety, and crypto management in practical, real-world terms. This chapter is essential for anyone holding digital assets like **Texit Coin (TXC)**.

# CHAPTER 6 — WALLETS: HOT, COLD, AND SECURE

## What Is a Wallet in Crypto?

A **crypto wallet** is a digital tool that allows you to store, send, and receive cryptocurrency. But unlike a physical wallet full of cash, a crypto wallet doesn't actually store the coins themselves.

Instead, it stores your **private keys** — the secret codes that give you access to your digital assets.

Think of it like a **key to your digital vault**. Whoever has that key, controls the money.

## Hot Wallets vs Cold Wallets

There are two major types of wallets:

### 🔥 Hot Wallets (Online)

A **hot wallet** is connected to the internet. Examples include:

- Mobile apps (e.g., Trust Wallet, Blockchain Mint)
- Desktop wallets
- Web-based wallets
- Exchange accounts (like BitMart or DexTrade)

**Pros:**

- Fast and easy to use

- Convenient for trading and transfers

**Cons:**

- Vulnerable to hacking

- Less secure for long-term storage

### Cold Wallets (Offline)

A **cold wallet** is completely offline — making it the most secure way to store crypto. It's typically a hardware device, USB stick, or even a physical coin with encrypted QR codes (like TXC's **Cold Storage Coin**).

**Pros:**

- Totally secure from online attacks

- Ideal for storing large amounts or long-term holdings

**Cons:**

- Less convenient for frequent use

- If lost, recovery may be impossible

## My Experience With Cold Storage

When I bought into the TXC mine, I received:

- **1 Tether Wallet**

- **2 Bitcoin Wallets**

- **1 Cold Storage Coin** for TXC

- Access to an entire community of miners along with live zoom meetings including Bobby Gray, the founder, as well as other leaders of the organization

That coin came via mail, and on the back was a QR code. I scanned it with the **Blockchain Mint app**, and instantly saw my TXC balance appear.

Here's the important part:

**Once you open a cold wallet, it's no longer secure.**

I'm currently waiting on a new cold wallet. Once I receive it, I'll:

1. Move my TXC to **Tether** (a stablecoin).

2. Transfer the long-term portion back to the new cold wallet.

3. Cash out the rest via an exchange.

It's a bit of a process, but it's simple and fast once you understand the flow.

## What Is a Stablecoin?

A **stablecoin** is a type of cryptocurrency whose value is tied to a real-world asset, usually the U.S. dollar. The most popular stablecoin is **Tether (USDT)**.

Here's why stablecoins matter:

- They **hold steady value** (unlike volatile coins like Bitcoin)

- They make it easier to **move money in and out** of crypto

- You can use them as a **bridge** between coins or exchanges

## Why Cold Storage Matters

Let's get serious: crypto can be hacked. If your wallet is online and you don't have strong protections, you could lose everything.

That's why TXC's model of sending **cold storage coins** is so powerful. It's one of the safest delivery methods in crypto — especially for newcomers.

If you lose your cold wallet or the QR code is compromised, **your TXC is gone forever**. So protect it like you would your passport or cash.

**"KEEP THIS COIN SAFE. IF YOU LOSE IT, YOUR $TXC WILL BE GONE!!!"**

## Summary: How to Handle Your Wallet Like a Pro

| Step | Action |
|:---:|---|
| 1 | Receive or buy your cold wallet |
| 2 | Download the **Blockchain Mint** app |
| 3 | Scan the QR code on the coin |
| 4 | Track your TXC balance in real time |
| 5 | When needed, move funds to a **stablecoin** like Tether |
| 6 | Re-store long-term funds in a **new cold wallet** |
| 7 | Cash out or reinvest with peace of mind |

**Tools You'll Need**

- ✅ **Blockchain Mint App** (iOS & Android)

- ✅ Access to a stablecoin wallet (Tether, USDC)

- ✅ A secure location for your cold coin

- ✅ Optional: Desktop wallet for advanced control

**Coming Up Next: Chapter 7 – Tracking, Trading, and Transferring Your $TXC**

You've mined your TXC. You've stored it safely. Now, how do you **track its value**, **transfer it**, or **cash it out**?

In the next chapter, we'll walk through how to:

- Monitor the price of your TXC

- Move funds between wallets

- Use TXC in real life

- Convert TXC to other coins or dollars

Ready to move on to **Chapter 7: Tracking, Trading, and Transferring Your $TXC**?

Awesome — let's keep the momentum going. In **Chapter 7**, you'll learn how to actively manage your Texit Coin: check its value, transfer it between wallets, and eventually convert it into other currencies or cash.

# CHAPTER 7 — TRACKING, TRADING, AND TRANSFERRING YOUR $TXC

## From Mining to Movement

Now that your TXC is safely stored — either in a **cold wallet** or **Tether wallet** — it's time to learn what comes next.

This chapter is all about **understanding how to manage your coin**:

- How much is it worth?

- How can you move it?

- How do you trade it for other coins or cash?

## Tracking Your $TXC Value

The value of TXC changes over time based on:

- Market demand

- Coin supply

- Public adoption and utility growth

As of late 2025, TXC has:

- Launched officially in **March 2025**

- Traded at **$0.028 in May 2025**

- Risen steadily to around **$1.00 per coin**

To check your balance and track TXC's value, use the:

✅ **Blockchain Mint App**

This mobile app allows you to:

- Scan the QR code on your cold wallet

- See real-time updates of your TXC balance

- Track your coin as the value rises

- Monitor mining output if you're part of the mine

It's like having a digital vault and a live coin tracker in your pocket.

**Pro Tip:** Even if you're not ready to trade or transfer, checking your coin value regularly helps you stay engaged and informed.

## Transferring Your Coin

Eventually, you may want to:

- **Move TXC from your cold wallet to Tether**

- **Send TXC to a friend or family member**

- **Cash out some of your coin for dollars** Here's a simple flow of how that process works:

## 1 Moving TXC to Tether (Stablecoin)

Why move to Tether?

- To **lock in value**

- To prepare for trading or withdrawal

- To avoid volatility if the market shifts

You can transfer TXC from your cold wallet to a wallet that supports **Tether (USDT)** — which acts like digital cash.

## 2 Cashing Out or Reinvesting

Once your TXC is in Tether, you have options:

- **Sell it on an exchange** like BitMart or DexTrade for dollars or other coins.

- **Transfer to your bank account** (requires identity verification on some exchanges).

- **Reinvest into another cold wallet** to continue holding long-term.

## 3 Using Your Coin in the Real World

TXC's ultimate mission is **real-world use**. As of now:

- The **City of Gonzales, Texas** is the first to begin the rollout.

- More cities and businesses are expected to follow.

- You may soon be able to use TXC for:

  o    Local services

  o    Business transactions

  o    Community programs

## Exchanges That Support $TXC

To trade or cash out, use a supported exchange:

- ✅ DexTrade

- ✅ MEXC

- ✅ BitMart

These platforms allow you to:

- Trade TXC for other coins (like BTC, ETH, or USDT)

- Withdraw funds to fiat currency

- Monitor price charts and volume

**Note:** You'll need to create an account and complete any necessary identity verification on these platforms.

### Common Tools for Transfers

| Tool | Purpose |
|---|---|
| **Blockchain Mint App** | Balance check, QR scanning |
| **Tether Wallet (USDT)** | Stable transfer or trade |
| **Exchange Account** | Buy, sell, or cash out |
| **Desktop Wallet** | Advanced control and storage |
| **Telegram Support** | Ask for help or troubleshooting |

### How to Buy Texit Coin (TXC) Without Mining: A Step-by-Step Guide

### Step 1: Set Up a Digital Wallet

- Download a crypto wallet such as:
    - MetaMask
    - Trust Wallet
    - Coinbase Wallet

- Follow the setup instructions and securely store your 12-word recovery phrase.

- Ensure your wallet supports the blockchain that Texit Coin uses (e.g., Ethereum or Binance Smart Chain).

**Step 2: Acquire Exchangeable Cryptocurrency**

- Purchase USDT, USDC, ETH, or BNB via:
    - Centralized exchanges (Coinbase, Binance, Kraken)
    - Debit/credit card or bank transfer

- Transfer your crypto to the wallet address from Step 1.

**Step 3: Find a Platform That Sells Texit Coin (TXC)**

- Identify where TXC is listed:
    - Decentralized exchanges (DEX) such as Uniswap or PancakeSwap
    - Official Texit Coin swap site or partner platforms

- Always verify the exchange's legitimacy.

**Step 4: Connect Your Wallet to the Exchange**

- Visit the exchange's website
- Click "Connect Wallet" and choose your wallet type (e.g., MetaMask)
- Authorize the connection inside your wallet app

**Step 5: Swap for Texit Coin (TXC)**

- Choose the crypto you have (e.g., USDT)
- Select TXC as the token to receive
- Input the amount you wish to swap

- Adjust slippage tolerance if needed

- Confirm and execute the transaction

## Step 6: Confirm Receipt of TXC

- After confirmation, check your wallet

- If TXC doesn't appear automatically: ◦ Add the token manually using the official contract address from the Texit Coin website

## Step 7: Secure Your Investment

- Backup your wallet and recovery phrase

- Consider transferring funds to a hardware wallet for safety

- Track your TXC using apps like:
  ◦ CoinGecko
  ◦ CoinMarketCap
  ◦ Blockfolio

**Reminder:** Always double-check token contract addresses and exchange links. Crypto transactions are irreversible. Practice caution and stay informed.

## Stay Informed While You Manage

Because TXC is evolving quickly, the **best way to stay current** is through Telegram:

- 📢 TEXITcoin Announcements – Official news

- 👥 mineTXC Chat – Community chat (members only)

- 💬 Support Channel – For help and guidance

- 📲 Personal Contact – ReardenMetals

Make sure to subscribe and check notifications — when a major price spike or usage update happens, you'll want to act fast.

## Recap: You're in Control

You're now a **crypto owner and miner** with tools to track, transfer, and trade your TXC. Here's what to remember:

- ✅ Use the Blockchain Mint App to track your coin

- ✅ Move to Tether if you're preparing to sell

- ✅ Use supported exchanges for trading or withdrawal

- ✅ Protect your wallet keys and cold storage devices

- ✅ Stay plugged into Telegram and email updates

**Coming Up: Chapter 8 – Staying Connected, Staying Ahead**

In the next chapter, we'll talk about the **biggest advantage in crypto**: staying in the loop. You don't have to be a tech genius to succeed — you just need to stay informed.

Let's talk community, alerts, updates, and how to catch the next big TXC move before it happens.

Now continuing to **Chapter 8: Staying Connected, Staying Ahead**?

Let's move forward with **Chapter 8**, where we focus on one of the most underrated aspects of success in crypto: **staying connected**. In a fast-moving environment like cryptocurrency, being informed early can make all the difference between watching from the sidelines and riding the wave.

# CHAPTER 8 — STAYING CONNECTED, STAYING AHEAD

## Crypto Moves Fast — Stay in the Loop

In traditional finance, major news cycles take days or weeks to impact your bank account. In crypto? **Minutes.** Sometimes even seconds.

Whether you're holding, mining, or preparing to trade, **staying informed** is critical. Fortunately, the Texit Coin ecosystem is designed to keep you in the know — with fast, secure communication channels and community support.

"You've got your seat on the rocket ship — now pay attention to when the boosters kick in."

## The Most Important Tool: Telegram

In crypto, **Telegram** is where the serious conversations happen. It's where updates break, where insiders connect, and where communities build. If you're not already on Telegram, now's the time.

Here are the four must-join channels for TXC:

1. 📢 **TEXITcoin Announcements**

   Stay ahead of market moves, partnership news, and official coin updates.

   👉 https://t.me/texitcoin_txc

2.  👥 **mineTXC Chat** (Members Only)

    Ask questions, meet fellow miners, and share tips.

    👉 https://t.me/+KWJExWOjuY9iMTQx

3.  🛠 **Blockchain Mint Support**

    Having issues with your wallet? Need help moving coins? Ask here.

    👉 https://t.me/blockchainmint

4.  💬 **Core Personnel Contact – ReardenMetals**

    Connect directly with a core team member for help or insight.

    👉 https://t.me/ReardenMetals

## Email Updates

TXC also sends key updates via email — especially around:

- New partnerships (like the rollout in Gonzales, TX)

- Mining system upgrades

- Wallet enhancements

- Exchange listings

- Time-sensitive calls to action

**Don't ignore your inbox**. If you've signed up for TXC, keep an eye on communications from the team.

## Real World Rollout – Gonzales, Texas

This isn't just theory. **Gonzales, Texas** is the first city to begin using **TXC as real currency**.

That means TXC isn't just a digital asset — it's becoming **usable money**. As the first "utility coin" in Texas, this move sets the precedent for other cities and counties to follow.

Being part of this now means you're **ahead of the wave**.

## Why This Matters

By staying plugged in, you'll:

- Be among the **first to hear of price jumps**

- Know when to **cash out, reinvest, or upgrade wallets**

- See **early announcements** about usage in new cities

- Get invited to **exclusive opportunities**, bonuses, or events Remember: **Knowledge = Profit** in the world of crypto.

## Suggested Habits for Staying Ahead

| Habit | Why It Matters |
| --- | --- |
| ✅ Join Telegram | Real-time updates and community support |
| ✅ Check the Blockchain Mint App | Track TXC balance and mining output |

| ✅ Read team emails | Avoid missing big announcements |
|---|---|
| ✅ Visit help.mineTXC.com | Stay sharp with guides, FAQs, and wallet setup info |
| ✅ Talk to other holders | Learn faster by asking questions and comparing notes |

**Coming Next: Chapter 9 – The Big Picture: TXC as a Utility Coin**

You've learned how to mine, store, track, and trade your TXC. Now let's zoom out and look at the **larger mission**.

In the next chapter, we'll explore:

- Why TXC isn't just a coin — it's a **movement**

- What it means to be a **utility coin**

- How TXC could change the future of **local economies in Texas**

- Where this project is heading next — and how you can play a part

In **Chapter 9: "The Big Picture – TXC as a Utility Coin"** we zoom out and explore the bigger vision behind Texit Coin (TXC). This is where the purpose comes into focus: it's not just about profits or tech — it's about power, independence, and local economic control.

# CHAPTER 9 — THE BIG PICTURE: TXC AS A UTILITY COIN

## More Than a Coin — It's a Cause

Cryptocurrency started as a response to centralized control. **Bitcoin** was born out of the 2008 financial crisis, offering an alternative to banks and governments. **Texit Coin** follows in that spirit — but with a **Texas-sized twist**.

TXC isn't just a coin you mine and sell. It's a **utility coin**, designed from the ground up to be **used like cash** — starting with **local economies in Texas**.

This is where the name *TEXIT* comes into full focus.

## What Is a Utility Coin?

A **utility coin** is a cryptocurrency that's created to **serve a practical function** — not just act as a speculative asset.

In the case of TXC, the utility is clear:

- To **spend like money**
- To **circulate in local Texas economies**
- To **give people financial tools outside of centralized control**

Utility coins are the future of **crypto-as-currency**, not just crypto-as-investment.

## Why Texas? Why Now?

Texas has always had a fierce streak of independence. The TXC project taps into that spirit with a bold vision:

**"What if Texas didn't just want to talk about economic independence… but build it — starting with its own money?"**

With inflation rising, distrust in centralized banks growing, and more people turning to alternative assets, TXC tpositions itself as **a financial lifeline** for communities who want more control over their economic destiny.

## Gonzales, TX – Ground Zero

The first city to officially explore TXC as usable money is **Gonzales, Texas** — a town famous for another revolutionary statement:

🏴 **"Come and Take It."**

Fitting, right?

In Gonzales, city leaders are working with the TXC team to begin accepting and circulating the coin. This is the **first pilot program** of many, and it shows that TXC isn't just theory — it's in motion.

Imagine:

- Paying for utilities in TXC
- Buying local groceries with TXC
- Earning a paycheck in TXC

That's the endgame — and it's starting now.

# The Long-Term Vision

Here's what the future could look like if TXC continues to grow:

| Stage | Goal |
|---|---|
| ✅ **Phase 1** | Build and operate the mine, grow coin supply |
| ✅ **Phase 2** | Launch coin and open trading on exchanges |
| ✅ **Phase 3** | Introduce cold storage wallets & tracking tools |
| ✅ **Phase 4** | Begin real-world use with pilot cities (like Gonzales) |
| ➡️ SOON **Phase 5** | Onboard new cities, local businesses, and vendors |
| ➡️ SOON **Phase 6** | Create decentralized community markets across Texas |

# A Community-Powered Economy

Unlike a government-backed fiat currency, TXC is:

- **Crowd-funded** through mining shares

- **Community-owned** by its participants

- **Transparent and public** on the blockchain

- **Built for Texans, by Texans** — but open to anyone who supports the cause It's more than a coin — it's a **new way to participate** in your own local economy.

## What This Means for You

If you're already a miner or holder of TXC:

- You're early.

- You're positioned to benefit as utility adoption increases.

- You're part of a movement that's **bigger than crypto** — it's about sovereignty, local empowerment, and real freedom.

## Stay Ready

The momentum is building. The team is moving fast. Cities are watching. If you're in this early, **you have a front-row seat** to one of the most ambitious grassroots financial projects in America today.

"There are optional things you can do — but for now, just sit back, stay connected, and enjoy the ride."

## Recap: Why TXC as a Utility Coin Matters

| Reason | Why It Matters |
|---|---|
| ✅ **Local Usage** | Meant to replace fiat for local spending |
| ✅ **Layer 1 Blockchain** | Built from the ground up for real utility |
| ✅ **Community Control** | You own the mine, the coin, and the outcome |
| ✅ **Piloting in Gonzales** | Real-world usage is already starting |
| ✅ **Transparency & Trust** | Public, trackable, and not a mystery project |
| ✅ **Aligned with Texas values** | Independence. Ownership. Legacy. |

**Final Chapter Coming Up: Chapter 10 – Your Role in the Future of TXC**

In our final chapter, we'll bring everything together:

- What you've learned

- What you can do next

- How to grow your role

- What to expect in the next 12 months of this journey

Ready for the next chapter? Shall we go to **Chapter 10? – Understanding Decentralized Exchanges and Liquidating Texit Coin**

# CHAPTER 10 – UNDERSTANDING DECENTRALIZED EXCHANGES AND LIQUIDATING TEXIT COIN

## What Are Apps Like DexTrade?

Apps like **DexTrade** are decentralized exchange platforms (often called DEXs) that allow users to trade cryptocurrencies directly from their wallets without relying on a central authority. Unlike traditional exchanges, which act as intermediaries and hold your funds, decentralized exchanges enable peer-to-peer trading on blockchain networks, giving users full control over their assets.

DexTrade is an example of such an app where you can swap various tokens, including Texit Coin, quickly and securely. These platforms typically offer:

- **Non-custodial trading:** You keep your private keys and funds at all times.

- **Smart contract execution:** Trades are executed through automated smart contracts, ensuring transparency and reducing risks.

- **Wide token availability:** Support for a wide range of cryptocurrencies and tokens, including new and niche projects like Texit Coin.

## What Is Coinbase?

**Coinbase** is one of the most popular centralized cryptocurrency exchanges globally, known for its user-friendly interface and security. It allows users to buy, sell, and store major cryptocurrencies like Bitcoin, Ethereum, and USDT (Tether). Unlike DEXs, Coinbase holds users' funds and offers additional services like fiat currency deposits and withdrawals, making it a popular choice for converting cryptocurrencies into traditional money.

## How to Liquidate Texit Coin into USDT and Withdraw to Your Bank Account

Liquidating Texit Coin into USDT (a stablecoin pegged to the US Dollar) and then transferring the proceeds to your bank involves several steps. Here's a clear step-by-step guide:

**Step 1: Transfer Texit Coin to a Supported Exchange (DexTrade or Centralized Exchange)**

- If Texit Coin is primarily traded on decentralized platforms like DexTrade, first connect your wallet to DexTrade.

- Swap your Texit Coin for USDT on DexTrade by selecting the appropriate trading pair (Texit/USDT).

- Alternatively, if Texit Coin is listed on a centralized exchange (e.g., Coinbase or Binance), deposit your Texit Coin there.

**Step 2: Swap Texit Coin for USDT**

- On DexTrade or the exchange platform, execute a trade to convert your Texit Coin to USDT.

- Confirm the transaction and wait for the blockchain confirmation.

**Step 3: Transfer USDT to a Centralized Exchange (If You Used DexTrade)**

Once you have swapped your Texit Coin for USDT on a decentralized exchange like DexTrade, the next step is to **move those USDT tokens to a centralized exchange** that allows you to convert them into fiat currency (such as USD) and withdraw to your bank account.

Here's a **step-by-step breakdown** of how to do this safely and correctly:

### 3.1: Choose a Centralized Exchange That Supports Fiat Withdrawals

You'll need to create an account (if you don't have one already) on a reputable exchange such as:

- **Coinbase** (supports fiat withdrawals to bank accounts in the U.S., U.K., EU, etc.)
- **Binance** (global, but varies by region)
- **Kraken**
- **Crypto.com**

Make sure the exchange **supports both USDT deposits and fiat withdrawals to your country**.

### 3.2: Locate Your USDT Deposit Address

Once your account is created and verified:

1. Log in to the centralized exchange (e.g., Coinbase).
2. Navigate to the **"Assets"** or **"Wallet"** section.
3. Find **USDT (Tether)** in the list of cryptocurrencies.
4. Click **"Deposit"** or **"Receive"**.
5. Choose the **correct network** for your USDT (e.g., Ethereum – ERC-20, Tron – TRC-20, or Binance Smart Chain – BEP-20).

   ⚠️ **Warning:** Using the wrong network can result in permanent loss of funds.
6. Copy your **USDT deposit address**.

### 3.3: Send USDT from Your Wallet (Used with DexTrade) to Your Exchange Account

Now go back to the wallet you used to trade on DexTrade (such as MetaMask, Trust Wallet, or a hardware wallet ex. Texit Coin via back office):

1.  Open your wallet and go to the **USDT balance**.

2.  Tap **"Send"** or **"Transfer"**.

3.  Paste the **USDT deposit address** from the centralized exchange.

4.  Select the **network** that matches the one used by the exchange.

5.  Enter the amount of USDT to send.

6.  Double-check all details. **It's critical** to match the network and address correctly.

7.  Confirm and authorize the transaction.

8.  Wait for the blockchain confirmation (this usually takes a few minutes but may vary depending on network traffic).

### 3.4: Verify Deposit on Centralized Exchange

After sending the USDT:

*   Go to the **Deposit History** or **Transaction History** section of your centralized exchange.

*   Wait for the status to show as **"Completed"** or **"Available."**

Once confirmed, your USDT is now on the centralized exchange, ready to be sold for fiat currency.

### Step 4: Sell USDT for Fiat Currency

- Once your USDT arrives on the centralized exchange, sell your USDT for your preferred fiat currency (USD, EUR, etc.).

- Confirm the sale and ensure the fiat balance is available in your exchange account.

### Step 5: Withdraw Fiat Currency to Your Bank Account

- Link your bank account to the exchange (if not already linked).

- Initiate a withdrawal request from your exchange fiat wallet to your bank.

- Depending on your bank and exchange policies, the withdrawal can take anywhere from a few minutes to a few business days.

## How to Trade Texit Coin for Other Cryptocurrencies (e.g., Bitcoin)

Trading Texit Coin for other cryptocurrencies like Bitcoin is straightforward on most exchange platforms:

1. **Use a DEX or Exchange:** Connect your wallet to a DEX like DexTrade or log into a centralized exchange where Texit Coin is listed.

2. **Select the Trading Pair:** Choose the trading pair you want, such as Texit/BTC or even Texit/USDT. (See trading pair definition in glossary)

3. **Place a Trade:** You can place a market order to buy Bitcoin instantly using your Texit Coin or a limit order to set a specific price.

4. **Confirm and Execute:** Confirm your trade and wait for the transaction to complete. The BTC will then be credited to your wallet or exchange account.

Ready for the chapter 11, **"Building Your Mining Network and Maximizing Texit Coin Bonuses"?**

**Although many who get involved with Texit Coin may say at first that they just rather watch their mine grow and experience wealth building, the truth is that many change their mind once they experience the rewards behind the bonus programs. In this next chapter, you will learn how easy it is to build your mining network. Let's go!**

# CHAPTER 11 — BUILDING YOUR MINING NETWORK AND MAXIMIZING TEXIT COIN BONUSES

In the world of Texit Coin, building a team isn't just a strategy — it's a pathway to unlocking substantial passive income through a **binary compensation model**. As a miner, you have the opportunity not only to generate coins through your own activity, but also to benefit from those you refer, and even from the actions of those further down in your network.

Let's break it down.

## Understanding the Binary Structure

Texit Coin operates on a **binary team structure**, meaning that each miner can sponsor two direct referrals — **one on the left leg, and one on the right leg**. Everyone you bring in after that is placed further down in your organization under one of these two "legs," helping you and your team grow.

- A **leg** in this system refers to one side of your network. You have a **left leg** and a **right leg**.

- As your network expands, you earn **points and bonuses** based on activity within both legs.

- This binary structure promotes **teamwork**, as members benefit from the activity of others beneath them.

# 🔥 Texit Coin BOGO Offer (Buy-One-Get-One): Explained

**What Is the BOGO Offer?**

The **BOGO (Buy-One-Get-One-Free)** promotion allows a participant in the Texit Coin mining program, who satisfies Rapid Rewards Plan requirements (ex. 3L/3R), to receive **an additional mining share completely free** when they choose earning additional hash power in exchange for their $1000 commission.

NOTE: You can choose to receive your commission in USDC, TXC, or Hash power. So choosing hash power gets you 2 for 1 meaning $1000 turns into $2000 of hash power or 200mh/s.

## 📋 How It Works – Step-by-Step

1. **You can acquire more than the 9 seat maximum by earning a commission and choosing hash.**

2. **You earn a point in your sponsor benefits or cash potential.**

✅ This means you **double your mining power for the money**. **Hash is the key!**

## 💡 Why It's a Big Deal

- 🤑 **Instant ROI Boost:** You're immediately receiving 2 shares for the price of 1.

- 📈 **Faster Daily Earnings:** With two shares mining instead of one, your **daily TXC accumulation rate doubles**.

- 🤝 **Improve Playing Field:** $1000 commission gets 200 mh/s, $2000 commission gets 400 mh/s, and $3000 commission gets 600 mh/s

⚠️ **Terms & Conditions**

- This is a **limited-time promotion**, often launched during growth phases or network expansion periods.

- The **free share is automatically applied** once your payment is verified — no codes needed.

- The BOGO offer is the only other promotion besides the One-Two-Free, that can allow a greater than 9 seat max acquisitions.

🧬 **How BOGO Supports the Ecosystem**

The BOGO offer isn't just a giveaway — it's part of a **strategic growth mechanism**. By giving early users more mining power, the network:

- Builds a **stronger, decentralized mining pool**

- Increases **block validation capacity**

- Boosts **community engagement and network effect**

It's designed to **reward early adopters**, accelerate trust in the ecosystem, and **build long-term value** for both the participants and the coin.

⚠️ **IMPORTANT**: This promotion is current as of this book's publication. Due to its popularity, it may be replaced in the future with a new structure, such as:

- **Buy 5, Get 1 Free**

- **Buy 9, Get 2 Free**

Stay informed through official Texit Coin communications to ensure you understand the **current active promotion.**

## Promotions: One-Two-Free and Beyond

The **"One-Two-Free" offer** is a **referral-based bonus program** within the Texit Coin ecosystem designed to **reward early participants and encourage network growth**. Here's a clear breakdown of how it works:

### Texit Coin's "One-Two-Free" Offer: Explained

### The Concept

The "One-Two-Free" offer is a **limited-time incentive** where **you can receive a free mining share** (100mh) after directly sponsoring 3 people who each purchase a mining share of their own. So it is a direct sponsorship component to this hybrid binary compensation model. If this goal is accomplished within 30 days the bonus is increased to (200mh) of output power. This means that an entry-level miner can absolutely triple their output early on by adding 3 miners.

### How It Works – Step-by-Step

1. **You purchase** one mining share of Texit Coin (TXC) to qualify as a miner.

2. **You refer 3 new people** to the TXC shared mining program.

3. Each of those **3 people purchases** a mining share (same or higher value) within 30 days.

4. **You receive 200 hash power (That translates to points on your legs)— completely free.**

NOTE: *It's important to work with your team or sponsor to get your new referrals placed on correct legs as a strategy to possibly earn more hash or even cash. Sponsorship bonuses (1-2-Free) run parallel to the placement tree growth benefits (Rapid Rewards Benefit).*

*To explain how these two benefits run parallel, when you enter your back office first go to your dashboard and sign in. There is a tab called "Sponsor". If you have 3 referrals, achieved within 30 days, you qualify for the 100mh. Then go back to the dashboard, select placement, you'll find your name at the* *top of the tree with referrals listed under you. There is a right leg and a left leg pointing downward. If you have 3 points on the right and 3 points on the left, you qualify for the Rapid Rewards bonus ($1000 cash, coins, or hash power).*

## What You Gain

| ◆ Action | ◆ Result |
|---|---|
| Buy 1 share | Begin mining TXC |
| Refer 3 who buy in 30 days | Earn 2 **additional points for free** |
| Repeat the cycle | Compound your mining power |

## Why It's Powerful

- ✅ **No additional cost to you** once you've referred two

- ✅ **Doubles your mining rewards** potential without more out-of-pocket expense

- ✅ **Encourages team building**, which strengthens the decentralized mining network

- ✅ **Multiplies your ROI** (Return on Investment) over time

## Notes and Conditions

- The referrals must **buy equal or higher-level shares** than you did.

- The bonus share is typically **the same level as your original purchase**.

- Some offers are **time-sensitive** or subject to caps, so acting early is encouraged.

- The system uses a **binary structure**, meaning left/right placement matters for bonuses (covered in Chapter 11 of your manuscript).

## Example Scenarios: Earning $1,000 Bonuses

Let's explore how real-world situations could play out using the binary system.

### Scenario 1: Jerry's Balanced Team

- Jerry sponsors **Susan, Billy, and Karen** on his **left leg**.

- He sponsors **Mike, Lisa, and Greg** on his **right leg**.

- All 6 individuals purchase **one share each**.

✅ Jerry earns the **$1,000 Cash Rapid Rewards bonus** — he can choose between $1,000 in USDT placed on his etherium cold storage coin, 1 free mining share, or additional Texit Coins.

### Scenario 2: Susan's Strategic Referrals

- Susan refers **9 new miners** on her **left leg**, each purchasing **1 share**. This is now her power leg.

- On her **right leg**, she sponsors **John, Amber, and Drew**, and each of them purchases **3 shares**.

✅ Total: 9 shares on one side, 9 shares (3 × 3) on the other.

🎉 This qualifies Susan for the **maximum bonus of $3,000** under the Rapid Rewards bonus system.

📌 Note: The weekly bonus **caps at $3,000** and does **not carry over**.

**Scenario 3: Billy's Tiered Growth**

- Billy brings in **2 people on his left** (each buying 3 shares) and **3 on his right** (each buying 1 share).

- Though it's not perfectly balanced, Billy has a match of 3 on the left and 3 on the right.

✅ He still qualifies for a Rapid Rewards bonus. he can choose between $1,000 in USDT placed on his etherium cold storage coin, 1 free mining share, or additional Texit Coins. It would be an enhancement if 6 more points could be achieved on the right leg brining him to the $3000 cap or Rapid Rewards equivalent.

💡 **Why It Aligns with Texit Coin's Mission**

The "One-Two-Free" offer reflects **community economics** — rewarding people not for hoarding crypto, but for **spreading access, education, and participation**. It's designed to make **crypto mining more inclusive and scalable**.

# Other Ways to Earn: Tier Sales and Limit Sales

Texit Coin also rewards miners for growing their network beyond the binary bonus:

✅ **Tier Sales**

- As your referred miners bring in others, **you earn from their activity**, even if you didn't directly refer those individuals.

- For example: If **Susan signs up Billy**, and **Billy signs up 6 more people**, Susan receives **tier commissions** and **binary points** from Billy's activity.

✅ **Limit Sales**

- At the time of the writing of this book, Texit Coin does not offer **limit sales bonuses**. However, limit sales does appear as an option when working with exchanges like Dex-Trade on open market transactions.

## Leg Structure and Strategic Planning

Understanding the strength of your legs is essential.

- If one leg grows faster than the other, it's called a **power leg**. Sometimes this is done as part of a strategy to maximize rewards.

- The slower-growing side is the **pay leg** — this is where you want to focus your new referrals to **unlock more bonuses**.

- The binary system requires **volume on both sides**, so balancing is key to consistent rewards.

## Final Thoughts: Consistency and Teamwork

Texit Coin's binary bonus system is designed to reward **strategic growth, team collaboration, and consistent effort**. Whether you're building a modest side income or aiming for the weekly $3,000 cap, your success depends on building **both legs of your binary tree** while helping your team do the same.

By referring miners, supporting their growth, and understanding the program's structure, you can unlock the full earning potential of the Texit Coin mining network.

**Pro Tip:** Always keep an eye on current promotions, weekly limits, and updated compensation rules through your dashboard or Texit Coin's official channels.

**Almost Final Chapter Coming Up: Chapter 12 – Your Role in the Future of TXC**

In our final chapter, we'll bring everything together:

- What you've learned

- What you can do next

- How to grow your role

- What to expect in the next 12 months of this journey

Ready for the last chapter? Shall we go to **Chapter 12 – Your Role in the Future of TXC**?

# CHAPTER 12 — YOUR ROLE IN THE FUTURE OF TXC

## You're Already In

By this point, you've done more than most:

- You understand what cryptocurrency is

- You've learned how mining works

- You know how to protect and manage your coin

- You've seen the real-world use case of TXC as a utility coin

- And best of all — **you own a piece of the mine**

This puts you on the **ground floor** of one of the most exciting crypto and economic experiments happening today.

But what comes next is just as important.

## What Can You Do Now?

Depending on where you are in the journey, here are the best next steps:

🔐 **If You Just Received Your Cold Wallet:**

- **Download the Blockchain Mint app**

- **Scan the QR code** to see your balance

- Keep your wallet **secure and offline**

- Ask support for help if needed: help.mineTXC.com

## ⚒ If You're Ready to Move or Trade:

- Convert some TXC to **Tether (USDT)** using a desktop or mobile wallet

- Use a supported exchange to **cash out or trade**:

   o   BitMart

   o   DexTrade

   o   MEXC

## 🔗 If You Want to Learn More:

- Join the **Telegram groups** to ask questions and learn from others

   o   Community: mineTXC Chat

   o   Updates: TEXITcoin Announcements

## 🚀 If You're Ready to Grow:

- **Buy more shares** of the mine to increase your daily coin output

- **Refer friends** and earn cash bonuses + mine power boosts

- Attend **local TXC events** or connect with other holders

## Watch for the Utility Rollout

The Gonzales, TX rollout is just the beginning. The next year may bring:

- More cities accepting TXC

- Vendor programs for small businesses

- Payroll and contract services using TXC

- Local commerce marketplaces running on the coin

**Stay connected**, and you'll be the first to know when opportunity opens.

## A Personal Note

Let me say this plainly:

**I know the founder of this project and the currency director personally.**

That matters. I've watched their commitment to transparency, integrity, and purpose. This isn't one of those "flash-in-the-pan" coins with anonymous devs and empty promises. It's **real people**, working to create **a real monetary alternative**that could transform local communities.

I'm not just telling you about this — **I'm living it.**

## Your Invitation to Build the Future

If you've ever wanted to:

- Take part in a financial revolution

- Help create a new economy

- Be early on something that actually matters

This is it.

**Texit Coin is an invitation to participate.**

Not just to profit — but to belong, to contribute, and to help shape what comes next.

## Final Checklist: Stay Active, Stay Secure, Stay Ready

✅ Cold wallet secure and scanned

✅ App downloaded and balance confirmed

✅ Tether account set up for liquidity

✅ Telegram channels joined for real-time news

✅ Help site bookmarked: help.mineTXC.com

✅ Exchange accounts created (BitMart, MEXC, DexTrade)

✅ Referred a friend or earned a bonus? Don't leave that on the table.

## Conclusion: The Ride Has Just Begun

You've got your seat on the rocket ship.

Whether you simply hold and watch your investment grow, or dive deep into building local adoption, you're now part of a **living, breathing, people-powered currency. Ok so I lied. I still have more to say following this part. Let's talk about a subject that many seem to avoid: Taxes! Let's also talk about how to buy things with your crypto. Now you're really onboard.**

# CHAPTER X — CRYPTO AND TAXES: WHAT YOU NEED TO KNOW (AND HOW TO KEEP MORE OF WHAT YOU EARN)

**Understanding Your Tax Responsibility**

When it comes to cryptocurrency, the IRS and many other global tax agencies now treat digital assets as **property**, not currency. That means every time you sell, trade, or spend your Texit Coin (TXC) — or any crypto — you could trigger a **taxable event**.

Here's what counts as a taxable event:

- **Selling crypto for cash**

- **Trading one crypto for another** (even if you don't convert to USD)

- **Using crypto to buy goods/services**

- **Receiving crypto as income or payment**

Each of these could lead to **capital gains tax** or **income tax**, depending on how the crypto was acquired and how long you held it.

**Types of Taxes You May Face**

- **Capital Gains Tax**: If you bought or mined TXC and later sold it at a higher value, the profit is taxed as a capital gain.

    o **Short-Term** (held < 1 year): taxed at your ordinary income rate

    o **Long-Term** (held > 1 year): taxed at a lower, favorable rate (typically 0%, 15%, or 20%)

- **Income Tax**: If you received crypto as payment, referral bonuses, or mining rewards, it may be taxed as income at the time you received it — based on its fair market value.

## Creative Strategies to Minimize or Eliminate Your Crypto Tax Burden

### 1. Hold Long-Term

The simplest method is to **HODL**. Holding your crypto for over a year turns short-term capital gains into long-term gains — often taxed at a much lower rate (or even zero if your income is under certain thresholds).

### 2. Offset Gains with Losses (Tax Loss Harvesting)

If you've lost money on one crypto investment, sell it to realize the loss and offset it against your gains in TXC or other cryptos. This can significantly reduce your tax bill and is perfectly legal.

### 3. Move to a Tax-Friendly State or Jurisdiction

U.S. states like **Texas, Florida, Wyoming, and Nevada** have **no state income tax** — meaning your crypto income may only be taxed federally. Some global jurisdictions (like Portugal or El Salvador) have **little to no tax on crypto** at all.

### 4. Use a Self-Directed IRA or Roth IRA for Crypto

With a self-directed IRA or Roth IRA, you can hold crypto **tax-deferred** (traditional IRA) or **tax-free** (Roth IRA). Gains inside the IRA are not taxed — and with a Roth, withdrawals in retirement are **completely tax-free**.

### 5. Gift Crypto to Family (Under Gift Limits)

You can legally gift crypto to others (such as family members) **up to $18,000 per person per year** (as of 2025) without triggering gift tax. This helps you transfer assets and potentially lower future tax liability.

6. **Donate Crypto to a Charity**

Donating appreciated crypto directly to a nonprofit not only avoids capital gains tax but also allows you to **deduct the fair market value** on your taxes — a win-win for generosity and smart planning.

7. **Use Stablecoins and Strategic Swaps**

Swapping your TXC to a stablecoin like USDT during market highs helps lock in gains, but you can also **strategically time the sale** for low-income years or when you have offsetting losses.

8. **Track Everything & Use a Crypto Tax Software**

Using tools like **CoinTracker, Koinly, or TaxBit** can help you optimize your strategy year-round. These apps sync with your wallets, track your cost basis, and generate IRScompliant reports — reducing errors and audit risk.

## ⚖️ Thoughts on Crypto Taxation

Smart tax planning is not about evading — it's about **strategizing legally**. With TXC's rising value, the time to prepare is **before** you sell or transfer.

As the ecosystem grows, new rulings and tools will emerge. Stay educated, consult with a **crypto-savvy CPA**, and consider working with legal or financial advisors who understand decentralized assets and blockchain-based finance.

After all, it's not just about what you earn — it's about what you keep.

# HOW TO BUY THINGS WITH CRYPTO DEBIT CARDS

## CRYPTO DEBIT CARDS

| | DASHDIRECT | BitPAY | coinbase |
|---|---|---|---|
| PRIMARY CRYPTO | | MULTIPLE | MULTIPLE |
| MULTI-COIN SUPPORT | | ✓ | 🔲 |
| CARD TYPE | | VIRTUAL & PHYSICAL | PHYSICAL & VIRTUAL |
| STAKING REQUIRED? | | ✗ | ✓ |
| REWARDS | | DISCOUNTS | ↓$↑ |
| | % DISCOUNTS | 0x | 2+% BACK |

Did you know that you could already totally live off your crypto holdings? Crypto debit cards work just like regular debit cards — but instead of pulling funds from a bank account, they pull from your cryptocurrency balance. These cards convert your crypto (like Bitcoin, Ethereum, or even Dash or USDT) into fiat (USD, EUR, etc.) at the point of sale, letting you spend your digital assets at millions of merchants worldwide.

## 🔥 Top Crypto Debit Card Options

### 🚀 1. DashDirect & DashDirect Mastercard

- **Purpose**: Built specifically for spending Dash (DASH) instantly.

- **Usage**: Offers a merchant directory for direct payments and a reloadable prepaid Mastercard.

- **Benefits**:

  ○ Often no conversion fees for DASH

  ○ Instant payments and discounts at major retailers

  ○ No bank required

- **Limitations**:

  ○ Primarily works with DASH, not other crypto assets

## 2. BitPay Mastercard

- **Purpose**: Spend multiple types of crypto, including Bitcoin, Ethereum, Litecoin, Doge, and stablecoins like USDC.

- **Benefits**:

  ○ Convert crypto to fiat at the time of transaction

  ○ No need to pre-load the card

  ○ App supports direct exchange between currencies

- **Differences**:

  ○ Works with a wide variety of coins

  ○ Offers spending notifications, and virtual or physical cards

- **Notes**: Requires identity verification (KYC), but **no staking required**

## 3. Coinbase Debit Card

- **Purpose**: Tied to your Coinbase account — spend directly from your crypto portfolio

- **Benefits**:
  - Supports multiple coins and stablecoins
  - Offers crypto rewards (e.g., get X% back in Bitcoin or XLM)

- **Drawbacks**:
  - Must be a verified Coinbase user (full KYC)
  - Some features require holding/staking Coinbase's own token (e.g., for fee reductions or increased rewards)

# 🔍 Key Terms Explained

### KYC – Know Your Customer

- A legal requirement for most crypto financial services
- Involves submitting personal information (ID, selfie, address)
- Used to prevent fraud, money laundering, and identity theft

### Can You Avoid KYC?

- Some **non-custodial wallets and crypto-only services** may let you transact without KYC
- However, **crypto debit cards from major providers** (BitPay, Coinbase, etc.) **always require KYC**
- DashDirect (app-based) sometimes allows non-KYC gift card purchases, but the Mastercard version requires verification

## ⚖️ Comparison at a Glance

| Feature | DashDirect | BitPay Mastercard | Coinbase Debit Card |
|---|---|---|---|
| **Primary Crypto** | Dash only | Many (BTC, ETH, USDC…) | Many (from Coinbase wallet) |
| **Multi-Coin Support** | ❌ | ✅ | ✅ |
| **Card Type** | Virtual/Physical | Physical & Virtual | Physical |
| **Staking Required?** | ❌ | ❌ | Sometimes (for rewards) |
| **KYC Required?** | Yes (for card) | Yes | Yes |
| **Direct Conversion?** | Limited | ✅ | ✅ |
| **Rewards Offered** | Discounts on DASH | No | Up to 4% crypto rewards |

## 🔄 Multi-Currency Exchange Perk (BitPay Highlight)

BitPay's biggest strength is its **built-in crypto-to-crypto or crypto-to-fiat conversion**. This means you can:

- Spend Bitcoin but be charged in USD

- Convert USDT to ETH and spend it

- Swap between stablecoins and major crypto on the fly

This is useful for managing price volatility or preserving profits while maintaining flexibility at the point of sale.

## Using Crypto Debit Cards to Buy This Book

Thanks to crypto debit cards like the **DashDirect Mastercard**, **BitPay Mastercard**, and the **Coinbase Debit Card**, purchasing this book with cryptocurrency is not only possible — it's seamless.

These cards function just like traditional debit cards but are funded by your crypto balance.

When you make a purchase, the card instantly converts your crypto (like DASH, BTC, or USDC) into fiat (USD) at the point of sale. That means you can buy this book from an online store, digital download page, or even in person — **as long as the vendor accepts Mastercard or Visa.**

**Here's How It Works:**

1. **Fund your crypto debit card**:

   o   If using BitPay, for example, load your card with Bitcoin or USDT.

   o   With Coinbase, your card automatically draws from your chosen crypto wallet.

2. **Visit the book's purchase page**: o The landing page will offer a "Buy Now" option via Stripe, PayPal, or other standard checkout gateways.

   o   Select **Mastercard** as your payment method.

3. **Use your crypto card like any normal card**:

   o   Enter your card number, expiration date, and CVV.

   o   The card provider handles the instant conversion behind the scenes.

4. **Confirmation and delivery**:

   o   Your transaction processes instantly.

   o   You receive either a printed version by mail or a digital copy by download/email.

**Why This Matters**

Buying this book with your crypto card isn't just about convenience — it's a statement. You're showing the world that **crypto isn't trapped in exchanges**. It's fluid. Spendable. Real.

You're also proving that **alternative financial tools work**, even in traditional marketplaces. No third-party censorship. No hidden restrictions. Just your money, your choice.

So whether you're loading USDC into BitPay or converting DASH via DashDirect, your journey into decentralized finance doesn't stop at holding tokens — **it lives through the purchases you make.**

## ← END Closing Thoughts

This book was never just about teaching crypto. It's about lighting a path forward.

You've seen how Texit Coin fits into a broader movement — one where **financial access, personal sovereignty, and decentralized power** aren't just buzzwords, but realities being built right now by people like you.

From wallets and mining rigs to DEXs and debit cards, this journey has equipped you with tools — not just for investment, but for **independence**.

## 🗽 Crypto Spending: A Statement of Financial Freedom

More than just a technical convenience, **spending with cryptocurrency is a powerful expression of freedom**. In a world where traditional financial systems can be weaponized to restrict access, **economic censorship becomes a quiet—but dangerous—violation of basic human rights**.

Crypto gives individuals the ability to **transact without gatekeepers**, to store value on their own terms, and to support causes, businesses, and communities that matter to them—**without asking permission**.

Whether you're buying coffee with Dash, booking flights with USDC, or purchasing this book with TXC, you're doing more than making a transaction — **you're exercising digital sovereignty**.

**That's why crypto is here to stay.**

This is just the beginning.

Now go stake your claim in the future. It belongs to builders, rebels, and dreamers.

It belongs to you.

# TEXIT QUICK PLAYBOOK

## USING METAMASK

**1** INSTALL THE EXTENSION

**2** CREATE A WALLET

**3** SECURE YOUR SEED PHRASE

**4** SEND AND RECEIVE FUNDS

**4** SEND AND RECEIVE FUNDS

## 1. Install the MetaMask extension (or mobile app)

| Desktop | Mobile |
|---|---|
| • Go to **metamask.io** and choose *Chrome*, *Edge*, *Firefox*, or *Brave*.<br><br>• Click **Add to [Browser]** → **Add Extension**. | • Open the **App Store** (iOS) or **Google Play** (Android).<br><br>• Search **"MetaMask"** (look for the fox icon) → **Install**. |

**Tip:** Pin the fox icon in your browser toolbar for quick access.

## 2. Create your wallet

1. Open MetaMask → click **Get Started** → **Create a Wallet**.

2. Choose a strong password (this locks MetaMask locally).

3. Accept the terms to continue.

## 3. Secure your Secret Recovery Phrase

1. MetaMask shows **12 words** in a specific order.

2. **Write them down OFF-LINE** (paper, metal seed plate).

3. Confirm the phrase by selecting the words in order.

4. Store it in a safe place—**never** email or screenshot it.

*Lose the phrase = lose the funds — no support can recover it.*

## 4. Add (or confirm) the correct network

If Texit Coin lives on a network other than Ethereum Mainnet (e.g., Binance Smart Chain):

1. Click the **network dropdown** (top center) → **Add network**.

2. Enter the RPC details provided by the Texit Coin docs (Network Name, RPC URL, Chain ID, Symbol, Block Explorer).

3. **Save**; MetaMask switches to the new network.

## 5. Add Texit Coin (TXC) as a custom token

1. Click **Assets** → **Import tokens**.

2. Paste the **official TXC contract address**. MetaMask auto-fills *Symbol* and *Decimals*.

3. **Add Custom Token** → **Import**. TXC balance appears under *Assets*.

## 6. Fund your wallet

| Receive (Deposit) | Send (Withdraw) |
|---|---|
| • Click **Account 1** → **Copy** to copy your wallet address. <br><br> • Paste this address on Dex-Trade (or the exchange you're using) in the *Withdrawal* field. <br><br> • Choose the correct network, enter the amount, confirm. | • Click **Send** in MetaMask. <br><br> • Paste the recipient's wallet address. <br><br> • Enter the amount of TXC or native coin (for gas), adjust **Gas Fee** if desired. <br><br> • **Confirm** → wait for on-chain confirmation. |

## 7. Connect wallet to Apps (e.g., Dex-Trade DEX)

1. On the dApp, click **Connect Wallet** → **MetaMask**.

2. MetaMask pops up: choose the account → **Next** → **Connect**.

3. You're now ready to swap, stake, or trade TXC directly.

## 8. Every-day security checklist

- **Seed phrase** → offline only.

- **Password** → unique; use a password manager.

- **Hardware wallet** (Ledger/Trezor) for > $1,000 value.

- **Phishing** → always check URLs; MetaMask will never DM you.

- **Back-ups** → keep duplicate seed phrase copies in separate secure locations.

# DEX-TRADE WALLET GUIDE:
# A STEP-BY-STEP WALKTHROUGH

## REGISTERING FOR A
## NEW DEX-TRADE ACCOUNT

1. Go to dex-trade.com

2. Click **"Sign Up"** at the top

3. Fill out the registration form

4. Click the link in the email to verify your address

### ◆ 1. Sign Up for a Dex-Trade Account

1. Visit dex-trade.com

2. Click the **"Sign Up"** button in the top-right corner.

3. Fill in the registration form:

    o   Email

   o   Password

   o   Confirm password

   o   Agree to terms

4. Click **"Sign Up"** again.

5. Check your email inbox and click the verification link to activate your account.

### ◆ 2. Make a Deposit into Your Wallet

1. Log in to Dex-Trade and go to **"Wallet"** → **"Deposit"**.

2. Use the search bar to find the cryptocurrency you want to deposit (e.g., USDT, BTC, TXC).

3. Click **"Generate Address"** next to the currency.

4. Copy the **deposit address** (or scan the **QR code**) to use it as the receiving address from your MetaMask or other exchange.

5. Send funds from your external wallet or exchange using that address.

⚠ **Important:** Double-check network compatibility (e.g., ERC-20, BEP-20).

### 3. Make a Withdrawal

1. Go to **"Wallet"** → **"Withdraw"**.

2. Choose the cryptocurrency to withdraw.

3. Paste the **recipient address** (e.g., Coinbase, MetaMask wallet address).

4. Enter the withdrawal amount.

5. Confirm via 2FA (two-factor authentication), if enabled.

6. Click **"Withdraw"** and wait for blockchain confirmation.

### 4. Trade Cryptocurrency

1. Navigate to **"Trade"** from the top menu.

2. Choose your trading pair (e.g., TXC/USDT).

3. Use the **Buy/Sell form**:

   o   Enter price (or select "Market" for instant).

   o   Enter amount.

   o   Review total and fee.

4. Click **Buy** or **Sell** to place the order.

5. Monitor your open orders and trade history in the lower panel.

### Extra Tips

- Always use **2FA** for added security.

- Check **Minimum Withdrawal Amounts** and fees before making withdrawals.

- Use the **Funds Transfer** tab if you want to move assets between different account sections (like Spot and Margin).

# 🔐 HOW TO SET UP TWO-FACTOR AUTHENTICATION (2FA) ON DEXTRADE

**What is 2FA?**

2FA adds an extra layer of protection to your Dex-Trade account by requiring a onetime code from your mobile device each time you log in or withdraw funds.

### STEP 1: Access Your Account Settings

1. Log into your Dex-Trade account.

2. Click on your **profile icon** (top right corner).

3. Choose **Settings** from the dropdown menu.

4. Look for the **Security** tab and click on **Enable 2FA**.

*This is where you begin the process of adding your authentication layer.*

### STEP 2: Enable 2FA in Dex-Trade

1. A QR code will be displayed on screen.

2. Dex-Trade will prompt you to **install a 2FA app** such as:

   ○ **Google Authenticator**

   ○ **Authy**

   ○ **Microsoft Authenticator**

These apps generate 6-digit time-sensitive codes used to log in securely.

### STEP 3: Scan the QR Code

1. Open your 2FA app and click **"+"** → **Scan QR code**.

2. Point your phone's camera at the QR code shown in Dex-Trade.

3. The app will save your Dex-Trade account and start generating 6-digit codes.

*You should now see a new entry labeled "Dex-Trade" in your 2FA app.*

## STEP 4: Confirm the Setup

1. Back in Dex-Trade, enter the **6-digit code** shown in your 2FA app.

2. Click **Verify**.

3. A green checkmark will confirm that your 2FA setup is complete.

You're now protected with 2FA! You'll be prompted to enter a new code every time you:

- Log in

- Make a withdrawal

- Change account settings

## Bonus Tips

- **Back up your 2FA recovery key** (usually shown beneath the QR code) — this can restore access if your phone is lost.

- For enhanced security, use an app like **Authy** that allows cloud backups.

- Never share your 2FA code with anyone — Dex-Trade support will never ask for it.

# HOW TO TRANSFER TXC BETWEEN YOUR WALLET AND DEXTRADE

**HOW TO TRANSFER TEXIT COIN TXC**

**1 COPY TXC ADDRESS**

← Wallet   Trade   Buy Crypto   (Settings)

1 Wallet
(Account 1)

Choose '2FA

**2 CHOOSE 'WITHDRAW'**

Paste     Amuonti address
Wallet address

**3**
Wallet address
Enter amount

**3 PASTE ADDRESS & ENTER AMOUNT**

4 PASTE ADDRESS & ENTER
TXC FRE  ✓

*Step-by-Step Instructions*

*Please note that before you attempt this process, you must convert your cold storage coin to hot storage on the Texit Coin back office.*

## ◆ Part 1: Transferring TXC To Dex-Trade (Deposit)

### ✅ Step 1: Log into Dex-Trade

- Go to dex-trade.com and log in.
- Navigate to Wallet → Deposit in the top menu.

### ✅ Step 2: Find TXC

- Use the search bar to find **TXC (Texit Coin)**.
- Click **"Deposit"** on the TXC row.

### ✅ Step 3: Copy Your TXC Deposit Address

- Dex-Trade will show your **TXC wallet address** and a **QR code**.
- Copy the address carefully, or scan the code from your wallet app.

### ✅ Step 4: Open Your Wallet (e.g., MetaMask)

- Open your wallet and make sure it's connected to the correct network (Ethereum, Binance Smart Chain, etc.).
- Click **Send** or **Transfer**.

### ✅ Step 5: Send TXC

- Paste the **Dex-Trade deposit address**.

- Enter the **amount of TXC** you want to send.

- Confirm the **network**, then approve and send.

### ✅ Step 6: Wait for Confirmation

- Allow a few minutes for the transaction to confirm on the blockchain.

- Check your Dex-Trade wallet to verify that TXC has arrived.

## 🔷 Part 2: Transferring TXC From Dex-Trade To Your Wallet (Withdrawal)

### ✅ Step 1: Log into Dex-Trade

- Click **Wallet → Withdraw**.

### ✅ Step 2: Select TXC

- Locate **TXC (Texit Coin)** using the search bar.

- Click **"Withdraw"**.

### ✅ Step 3: Enter Your Wallet Address

- Go to your personal wallet and **copy your wallet address**.

- Paste this into Dex-Trade's **recipient address** field.

## ☑ Step 4: Set Amount & Network

- Enter the amount of TXC you wish to withdraw.

- Confirm the correct **blockchain network** (e.g., BSC or Ethereum).

## ☑ Step 5: Enable 2FA (if not already done)

- Enter your **2FA code** to authorize the withdrawal.

## ☑ Step 6: Confirm & Monitor

- Click **Withdraw** and wait for the blockchain confirmation.

- TXC will appear in your wallet shortly.

## 🛡 Tips for Safe Transfers

- Always **double-check addresses**—copy/paste only.

- Be sure you're using the **correct network**.

- Bookmark dex-trade.com to avoid phishing sites.

- Never share your **private keys or seed phrase** with anyone.

# 💱 HOW TO BUY TEXIT COIN (TXC) ON DEX-TRADE

*Step-by-Step Guide for Market & Limit Orders*

## ◆ What's the Difference?

- **Market Buy**: You buy TXC instantly at the current market price.
- **Limit Buy**: You set your own price — the order fills only if TXC hits that price.

## 🟢 Part 1: Market Buy TXC (Instant Purchase)

### ✅ Step 1: Log into Dex-Trade

- Go to dex-trade.com
- Login and navigate to the **Trade** tab from the top menu.

### ✅ Step 2: Find the TXC Market

- In the search bar, type "**TXC/USDT**" (or TXC paired with your preferred currency).
- Click the pair to load the trading screen.

### ✅ Step 3: Set Up the Market Order

- Under the **Buy TXC** panel, switch from **Limit** to **Market**.
- Enter the **amount of USDT** you want to spend.
- The platform automatically calculates how much TXC you'll receive.

## ✅ Step 4: Confirm the Order

- Click **Buy TXC**.

- Check the confirmation message.

- Your TXC will appear in your Dex-Trade wallet under **Balances**.

## 🟡 Part 2: Limit Buy TXC (Price You Choose)

## ✅ Step 1: Repeat Login & Market Search

- Log into Dex-Trade, go to **Trade**, and search for **TXC/USDT**.

## ✅ Step 2: Use the Limit Buy Form

- Make sure the **Limit** option is selected (this is usually the default).

- Enter your **desired price per TXC**.

- Enter how many **TXC** you want to buy.

## ✅ Step 3: Review and Place the Order

- Review the **Total USDT** that will be spent.

- Click **Buy TXC**.

- Your order is now active and listed under **Open Orders** at the bottom of the screen.

### ✅ Step 4: Monitor or Cancel the Order

- If TXC's price hits your target, the order will automatically execute.

- If not, you can cancel the order anytime by clicking the **Cancel** button next to it.

### 🔗 Pro Tips

- **Market orders** are best when you need to buy quickly.

- **Limit orders** are best when you're targeting a better price and can wait.

- Use **stop-limit** for more advanced control (ask if you'd like a guide on that too).

- Always double-check amounts and network fees before confirming.

# 🔗 "LINK ETH COIN TO METAMASK ON IOS"

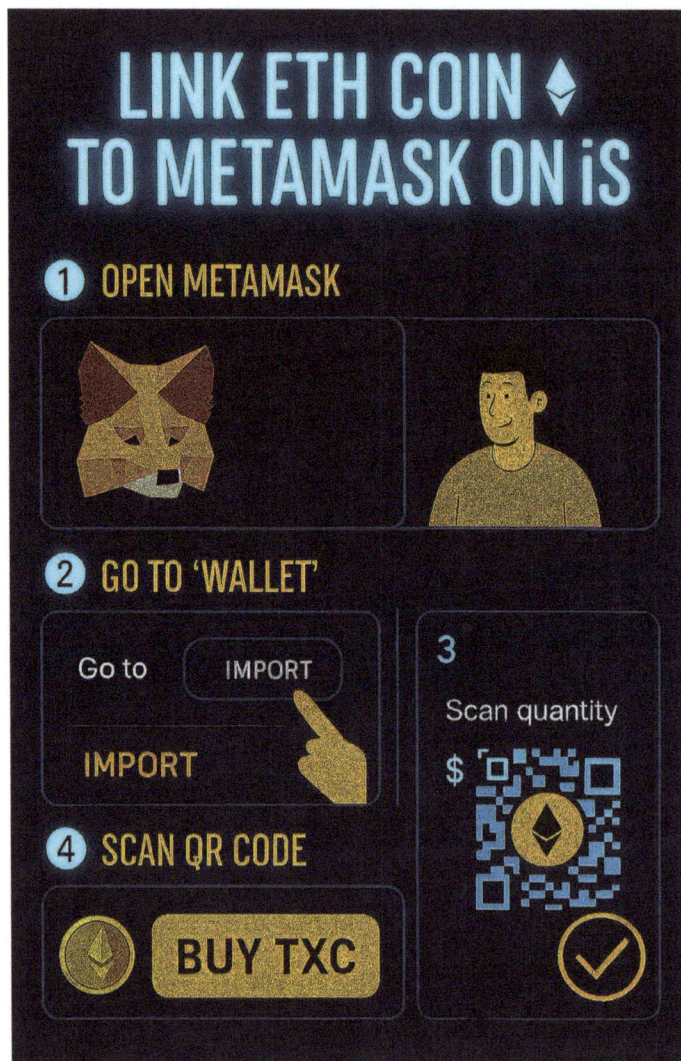

## LINK ETH COIN ♦ TO METAMASK ON iS

**1** OPEN METAMASK

**2** GO TO 'WALLET'

Go to   IMPORT

IMPORT

**3** Scan quantity
$

**4** SCAN QR CODE

BUY TXC

*How to connect your Ethereum (ETH) cold wallet to MetaMask on your iPhone*

### ◆ Step 1: Install the MetaMask App (iOS)

1. Open the **App Store** on your iPhone.

2. Search **"MetaMask"** and confirm it's from *MetaMask by ConsenSys*.

3. Tap **Download** and install the app.

### ◆ Step 2: Open MetaMask and Select "Import Wallet"

1. Open MetaMask after installation.

2. Tap **"Get Started"**, then select **"Import using Secret Recovery Phrase"**.

3. If you already have MetaMask set up and want to add another wallet:

   o   Tap the **Menu (!)** → **Settings** → **Wallets** → **Import Account**.

### ◆ Step 3: Enter Your ETH Cold Wallet's Secret Phrase or Private Key

1. If you're importing a **12-word recovery phrase**:

   o   Type the **exact order** of words with spaces.

2. If you have a **private key**:

   o   Choose "Import Account" → paste the private key in the box.

⚠️ *Do this only in a secure, private environment. Never share your key.*

### ◆ Step 4: Name the Wallet (Optional)

- After importing, you can assign a **nickname** to your wallet to help organize multiple accounts (e.g., "Cold Storage ETH").

### ◆ Step 5: Verify ETH Appears

1. Tap **Wallet** → you should now see your ETH balance.

2. If not:

   ○ Tap **"Import Tokens"**, then search for **ETH**.

   ○ Confirm your ETH token is linked and visible.

### 🔒 Security Best Practices

- Avoid storing private keys in digital notes or screenshots.

- Use MetaMask with a **Face ID lock** for added iOS protection.

- Consider transferring high-value ETH to a **hardware wallet** like Ledger or Trezor.

# HOW TO CONFIGURE COMMISSION PREFERENCES & ADD YOUR USDC PAYOUT ADDRESS

## SET YOUR COMMISSION & USDC ADDRESS IN TXC BACK OFFICE

**1** LOG INTO TXC BACK OFFICE

**3** NAVIGATE COMMISSION PREFERENCES

STATIC  DYNAMIC

**4** ENTER USDC wallet address

**4** ENTER USDC WALLET ADDRESS

**5** SAVE CHANGES

**SAVE**

◆ **Step 1 — Log into the TXC Back Office**

1. Go to **backoffice.texitcoin.com** (example URL).

2. Enter your **username / password** → click **Login**.

3. Complete **2FA** if enabled.

◆ **Step 2 — Open "Commission Settings"**

1. In the left-hand menu, click **Settings** → **Commission**.

2. A page titled **Commission Preferences** will appear.

◆ **Step 3 — Choose Your Commission Style**

| Option | What It Means | Typical Use Case |
|--------|---------------|------------------|
| **Static** | Fixed commission % on every sale (e.g., 5%) | You want predictable, flat earnings. |
| **Dynamic** | Tiered % based on volume or rank | You want higher payouts as your network grows. |

Toggle the switch to **Static** *or* **Dynamic** and set the desired percentage or tier.

◆ **Step 4 — Add Your USDC Wallet Address**

1. Below the commission section, locate **"USDC Payout Address."**

2. Copy your **USDC wallet address** (ERC-20 or BSC—match TXC's network).

3.   Paste the address in the field provided.

4.   Double-check for typos! Crypto withdrawals are irreversible.

## ◆ Step 5 — Save & Confirm

1.   Click **Save Changes**.

2.   You should see a green **"Success"** banner.

3.   Test by triggering a **small commission payout** (if available) or wait until the next cycle to verify USDC arrives in your wallet.

## 🛡 Best Practices

- **Network Match:** Be sure your USDC address is on the **same blockchain network** TXC uses for payouts.

- **2FA Required:** TXC back office will typically ask for your **2FA code** before saving withdrawal details—keep your authenticator app handy.

- **Periodic Review:** Revisit settings any time your commission plan changes or if you switch wallets.

# HOW TO IMPORT YOUR PHYSICAL TXC COIN INTO THE TXC WALLET APP (MOBILE)

CONNECT PHYSICAL TXC COLD STORAGE COIN TO TXC WALLET

STEP 1
OPEN THE TXC WALLET APP

TEXI COIN TEXAS CO

STEP 2
SCAN THE COIN'S QR CODE

STEP 4
VERIFY YOUR TXC BALANCE

0xA609.. DFZA
CONFIRM IMPORT

257.80

## ◆ What You Need

- The **TXC Wallet** mobile app (iOS or Android)

- Your **physical cold-storage Texit Coin** (QR sticker on reverse side)

- Optional: Pen & paper to note the private key for backup

## Step 1 — Open the TXC Wallet App

- Launch the **TXC Wallet** on your phone.

- Log in or create a new account if prompted.

## Step 2 — Scan the Coin's QR Code

1. On the wallet dashboard, tap **"Import Wallet"** (or **"Add Account"** → **"Scan QR"**).

2. Flip the coin and **scan the QR code** with your phone's camera.

   ○ The QR typically contains the **private key** or **WIF** for that coin.

## Step 3 — Confirm the Import

- The app will show a preview of the imported address.

- Tap **"Confirm Import"**.

- (Optional) **Label** the wallet (e.g., "Cold Coin #1") for easy tracking.

## Step 4 — Verify Your TXC Balance

- Return to the wallet dashboard.

- You should now see a new account with the **full TXC balance** stored on the coin.

- Tap the wallet to view the on-chain transaction history.

## Security Reminders

- Once imported, the TXC is **hot** (online) and no longer "cold."

- If you prefer to keep funds offline, **transfer** the TXC back out after viewing.

- Back up the coin's private key in a secure location (metal seed plate or fireproof safe).

# SWAP TEXIT COIN (TXC) TO USDT — STEP-BY-STEP

## HOW TO SWAP TEXIT COIN (TXC) TO USDT

**STEP 1**
OPEN THE DEX-TRADE OR TXC WALLET

**STEP 2**
SELECT TXC CONVERT TO USDT

CONFIRM SWAP

**STEP 4**
CHECK BALANCE

$52.40

### STEP 1 — Open the Dex-Trade App (or TXC Wallet with Swap Feature)

1. Log in to **Dex-Trade** on mobile or desktop.

2. Navigate to **Trade → Markets** (if using Dex-Trade) *OR* open the built-in **Swap** tab in the official **TXC Wallet** app.

### STEP 2 — Select the Trading Pair

- In the search bar, type **TXC/USDT** (for Dex-Trade) or choose **TXC → USDT** in the wallet's swap screen.

- Click the pair to load the trading form.

### STEP 3 — Enter Amount & Confirm Swap

| If using Dex-Trade | If using TXC Wallet |
|---|---|
| • Choose **Market** or **Limit**. <br><br> • Enter the **TXC** amount to sell. <br><br> • Review the **USDT you'll receive**. <br><br> • Click **Sell TXC / Buy USDT → **Confirm. | • Enter the TXC amount you wish to swap. <br><br> • Tap **Review Swap** → Check rate & fee. <br><br> • Tap **Confirm Swap** → Approve in-app. |

### STEP 4 — Check Your USDT Balance

1. Go to **Wallet → Balances** (Dex-Trade) or **Assets** (TXC Wallet).

2. Confirm the **USDT** amount appears.

3. Your TXC balance will decrease by the swapped amount.

## Tips & Notes

- **Network Fees:** Ensure you have enough native gas token (e.g., BNB or ETH) if swapping on-chain.

- **Slippage:** For large swaps, adjust slippage tolerance (1–2%) to prevent failures.

- **Security:** Enable **2FA** on Dex-Trade before swapping large amounts.

# HOW TO CASH OUT USDT TO USD (USING COINBASE OR SIMILAR EXCHANGES)

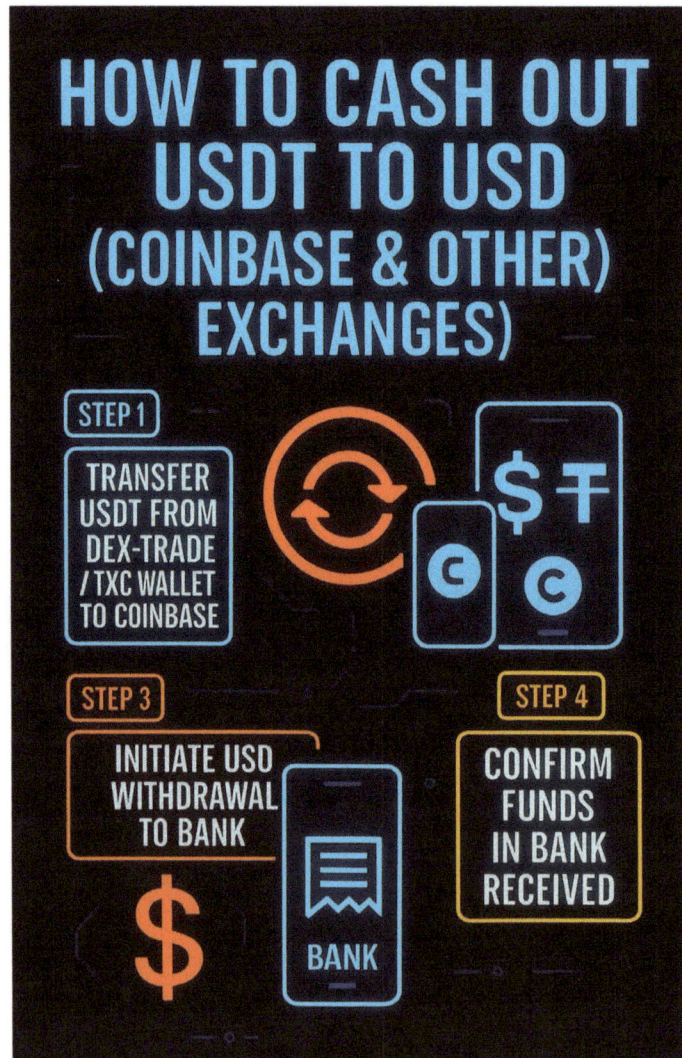

HOW TO CASH OUT USDT TO USD (COINBASE & OTHER) EXCHANGES)

STEP 1
TRANSFER USDT FROM DEX-TRADE / TXC WALLET TO COINBASE

STEP 3
INITIATE USD WITHDRAWAL TO BANK

BANK

STEP 4
CONFIRM FUNDS IN BANK RECEIVED

## Step 1 – Transfer USDT to Coinbase (or Kraken, Binance US, etc.)

1. Inside **Dex-Trade** or your **TXC Wallet**, go to **Withdraw → USDT**.

2. In Coinbase, tap **Receive → USDT (ERC-20 or TRC-20)** and copy the address (or QRscan it).

3. Paste that address in Dex-Trade, choose the correct network, enter the amount, and **Confirm**.

4. Wait for on-chain confirmation; the USDT will appear in your Coinbase balance.

## Step 2 – Convert / Sell USDT for USD

*Coinbase example*

1. Tap **Trade → Sell / Convert**.

2. Select **USDT → USD** (Convert) *or* choose **Sell USDT**.

3. Enter the amount; review fees and tap **Preview → Convert/Sell Now**.

4. USD instantly credits to your **USD wallet** inside Coinbase.

*(On Kraken, Binance US, or Gemini, use the **Spot Trade** screen and place a **Market Sell USDT/ USD** order.)*

## Step 3 – Withdraw USD to Your Bank

1. In Coinbase, open **Assets → USD → Cash Out**.

2. Choose **ACH (1-3 days, free)** or **Instant Debit Card** (fee applies).

3. Enter withdrawal amount → **Continue → Cash Out Now**.

4. Follow any 2FA prompts; funds will show in your bank per the method chosen.

## Step 4 – Verify Funds Arrived

- Check your **bank app** or online banking for the incoming deposit.

- Coinbase will mark the cash-out **Complete** when the transfer settles.

📌 **Tips & Best Practices**

| Tip | Why It Matters |
|---|---|
| **Match networks** (ERC-20 vs. TRC-20) when withdrawing USDT. | Sending on the wrong chain can permanently lose funds. |
| **Enable 2FA** on both Dex-Trade & Coinbase. | Prevents unauthorized withdrawals. |
| **Small test withdrawal** first time you off-ramp. | Confirms routing & fees before moving large sums. |
| **Check daily limits** on your exchange. | You may need to raise limits for high-value conversions. |

# APPENDIX & GLOSSARY: UNDERSTANDING CRYPTOCURRENCY TERMINOLOGY

This section is your quick-reference guide to the essential terms, platforms, coins, and tools used in the cryptocurrency world, including those specifically relevant to **Texit Coin** and modern digital asset ecosystems.

## A. Cryptocurrency Platforms, Apps, and Tools

| Name | Definition |
|------|------------|
| **Texit Coin** | A blockchain-based token with a binary structure for network building, mining, and trading. |
| **DexTrade** | A decentralized exchange (DEX) where users can swap tokens like Texit Coin directly. |
| **Coinbase** | A centralized, U.S.-regulated crypto exchange known for ease of use and fiat withdrawals. |
| **Binance** | The largest global crypto exchange by trading volume, offering thousands of trading pairs. |
| **Trust Wallet** | A mobile crypto wallet supporting many blockchains and tokens, often used with DEXs. |
| **MetaMask** | A browser extension and mobile wallet for Ethereum and other networks; popular for DeFi apps. |
| **Kraken** | A major U.S.-based exchange offering fiat on-ramps and advanced trading tools. |
| **Crypto.com** | A mobile-first crypto exchange offering Visa cards and DeFi features. |
| **Uniswap** | A leading Ethereum-based DEX for swapping ERC-20 tokens. |
| **PancakeSwap** | A DEX on the Binance Smart Chain (BSC), often used for trading new altcoins and tokens. |
| **Etherscan** | A blockchain explorer for Ethereum transactions and tokens. |
| **BSCScan** | A blockchain explorer for Binance Smart Chain transactions. |

## B. Popular Cryptocurrencies and Stablecoins

| Name | Symbol | Definition |
|---|---|---|
| **Bitcoin** | BTC | The first and most widely known cryptocurrency, considered digital gold. |
| **Ethereum** | ETH | A blockchain with smart contract functionality, powering DeFi and NFTs. |
| **Tether** | USDT | A stablecoin pegged to the U.S. dollar, commonly used for trading and liquidity. |
| **Texit Coin** | TEXIT | A decentralized coin with bonus structures, binary networking, and mining features. |
| **BNB** | BNB | The native token of Binance, used for trading fee discounts and DeFi apps. |
| **Solana** | SOL | A high-speed blockchain platform popular for DeFi and NFTs. |
| **Cardano** | ADA | A proof-of-stake blockchain focused on security and sustainability. |
| **XRP** | XRP | A token designed for fast and low-cost international payments. |
| **USD Coin** | USDC | A regulated stablecoin backed by fiat reserves, used for trading and DeFi. |
| **Polygon** | MATIC | A layer-2 scaling solution for Ethereum with fast, low-cost transactions. |

## C. Core Terms and Definitions

| Term | Definition |
|---|---|
| **Altcoin** | Any cryptocurrency other than Bitcoin. |
| **Blockchain** | A decentralized ledger that records transactions across a network of computers. |
| **Wallet** | A digital app or hardware device used to store private keys and manage cryptocurrency balances. |
| **Private Key** | A secure, secret code that allows access to your cryptocurrency. |
| **Public Address** | A string of letters and numbers where people can send you crypto. |

| Decentralized Exchange (DEX) | A peer-to-peer platform that allows users to trade without a central intermediary. |
|---|---|
| Centralized Exchange (CEX) | A platform where a company manages crypto trades, custody, and fiat transactions. |
| Smart Contract | Code that runs on a blockchain to automatically execute agreements without intermediaries. |
| Mining | The process of validating blockchain transactions and earning cryptocurrency as a reward. |
| Staking | Locking up cryptocurrency to support network operations and earn rewards. |
| Liquidity Pool | A pool of user-contributed tokens used to facilitate trading on DEXs. |
| Gas Fees | Transaction fees paid to blockchain validators (especially on Ethereum). |
| Token | A digital asset created on an existing blockchain, often used in DeFi apps. |

| NFT (Non-Fungible Token) | A unique digital asset that represents ownership of a specific item or artwork on the blockchain. |
|---|---|
| Stablecoin | A cryptocurrency pegged to the value of a real-world asset like the USD. |
| Fiat Currency | Government-issued currency such as USD, EUR, or GBP. |
| Cold Wallet | A wallet not connected to the internet, offering higher security (e.g., hardware wallet). |
| Hot Wallet | A wallet connected to the internet, typically used for frequent trading. |
| Peer-to-Peer (P2P) | Direct transactions between users without a central authority. |
| Centralized Cryptocurrency | A digital asset where **control is retained by a single entity or small group**, such as a company, development team, or founder. This entity manages key decisions, such as: Supply Issuance, Codebase Updates, Transaction Approval Mechanisms, and Go verance and Network Rules. **Examples**: XRP (Ripple), USDT (Tether), and many exchangeissued tokens like BNB (Binance Coin) |

| | |
|---|---|
| **Permissioned Blockchain** | Refers to the underlying blockchain structure of a centralized coin. In a permissioned system: Only selected nodes can participate in validating transactions. Access to the network is **restricted**, unlike public (permissionless) blockchains like Bitcoin or Ethereum. |
| **Custodial Cryptocurrency** | A coin that requires third-party custody, usually where the user doesn't control their private keys (e.g., coins stored in exchange wallets). |
| **Trading Pair** | Combinations of trade opportunities such as: Bitcoin/Etherium, Litecoin/Tether. Texitcoin/Bitcoin, Texitcoin/USDT. |
| **Global Index** | A metric or data source referenced for tracking TXC market health, user activity, and liquidity across exchanges. |
| **Tier 1 (Top Layer)** | This layer consists of **founders, early adopters**, and primary stakeholders. These members are often involved in strategic decisions and receive benefits from early mining, premium access, and foundational pools. |
| **Tier 2 (Builder Layer)** | Comprised of **active affiliates, team leaders**, and mid-level participants who engage in onboarding, education, or structured referrals. Tier 2 users are often rewarded through **commission overrides, dynamic bonuses**, or token multipliers. |
| **Tier 3 (Entry Layer)** | This is the **new participant or casual user** level. These users typically engage in token purchases, trading, or basic usage without taking on team-building or leadership roles. Incentives here are often static or activity-based. |
| **Tier 1 (Top Layer)** | This layer consists of **founders, early adopters**, and primary stakeholders. These members are often involved in strategic decisions and receive benefits from early mining, premium access, and foundational pools. |

## D. Texit Coin Specific Terms

| Term | Definition |
|------|------------|
| **Binary Structure** | A network compensation plan with two legs (left and right), where bonuses depend on balanced growth. |
| **Cash/BOGO Bonus** | A bonus earned when both legs of your network reach a certain number of active miners. |
| **Leg (Left/Right)** | One side of your binary network tree used to determine eligibility for team bonuses. |
| **Power Leg** | The stronger-performing leg in your binary team. |
| **Pay Leg** | The weaker-performing leg, used to calculate payouts. |
| **Tier Sale** | A bonus structure that pays miners when their team members sell packages at various levels. |
| **Limit Sale** | A structure that rewards miners based on reaching volume thresholds. |
| **Mining Share** | A purchased unit that enables users to generate Texit Coins over time. |
| **One-Two-Free Promo** | A referral promotion where referring two people may earn a free share. |
| **Buy 5 Get 1 / Buy 9 Get 2** | Future promotion structures replacing One-Two-Free, offering free shares at volume-based milestones. |
| **Weekly Bonus Cap** | Maximum of $3,000 in binary bonuses per week; bonuses do not roll over. |
| **Referral** | A person directly signed up under you in the binary system. |
| **Global Index** | A metric or data source referenced for tracking TXC market health, user activity, and liquidity across exchanges. |
| **Mining (TXC)** | Unlike traditional crypto mining, TXC uses structured incentives through community-based distribution and affiliate networks. |
| **Back Office** | The secure user dashboard where members manage their accounts, commissions, wallet addresses, and promotional tools. |

| TXC Cold Storage Coin | A physical coin containing a QR-coded private key that stores TXC securely offline. Can be imported into supported digital wallets. |
|---|---|
| Mission Control | The central operations and strategy unit for overseeing the Texit Coin platform, user activity, and economic structure. |
| Activation Fee | A one-time or recurring fee that enables access to full features of the TXC platform, including earnings and swaps. |
| Swap Portal | The internal or third-party DEX interface where users can exchange TXC for USDT or other supported tokens. |
| Smart Contract | Blockchain-based programming that executes the distribution of TXC, referral bonuses, or commissions. Users are encouraged to verify contract addresses. |
| USDC Address | The wallet address used by TXC platform members to receive commission payouts in USD Coin. Must match the correct network. |

## E. Trading & Liquidity Terms

| Term | Definition |
|---|---|
| Swap | Trading one cryptocurrency for another, typically via a DEX. |
| Slippage | The difference between expected and actual trade prices, often due to liquidity. |
| Pairing | Two assets that can be traded against each other, like TEXIT/USDT or BTC/ ETH. |
| Volume | The amount of cryptocurrency traded within a given period. |
| Order Book | A list of buy and sell orders for a specific trading pair. |
| Limit Order | An order to buy or sell at a specific price. |
| Market Order | An order to buy or sell immediately at the best available price. |

www.ingramcontent.com/pod-product-compliance
Lightning Source LLC
Chambersburg PA
CBHW052342210326
41597CB00037B/6228